Women and Men in the Qur'an

"In the midst of media and academia dominated discourses about Muslim women's discriminatory treatment, the present volume provides a scholarly interpretation of the Islamic primary sources to present women and also men as equal partners in the life dictated by modernist ideological expectations. Dr. Asma Lamrabet, without engaging in apologetics, has rendered a great service to women's cause by responding to the systematic denigration of women's stature and rights in Muslim sources, in order to reinstate the dignity and human worth of women in Islamic tradition. The classical exegetical materials are critically evaluated for their culturally biased position against women. The inclusive and even-handed approach to the question of gender discrimination in Muslim culture leaves the study free of the usual feminist polemics. Dr. Lamrabet's approach allows the Islamic sources to speak for themselves about controversial treatment of the gender disparity. Moreover, the author commendably presents the contemporary lip-service treatment of women's rights undertaken by Muslim political and religious leadership. The problems with governance in the Muslim world have done very little in reorienting Muslim traditional attitudes to the questions of justice and equality to improve the lot of the women today. Dr. Lamrabet has correctly concluded that without the democratic governance committed to promote the fundamental rights of all its citizens, especially of women, all talk of reform remains empty and unfulfilled in Muslim societies."

—Abdulaziz Sachedina, *Chair, Religious Studies, and Endowed IIIT Professor of Islamic Studies, George Mason University, USA*

Asma Lamrabet

Women and Men in the Qur'ān

Asma Lamrabet
L'hôpital Avicennes de Rabat
Rabat, Morocco

Translated by Muneera Salem-Murdock, Washington, DC, USA

ISBN 978-3-319-78740-4   ISBN 978-3-319-78741-1   (eBook)
https://doi.org/10.1007/978-3-319-78741-1

Library of Congress Control Number: 2018938336

Translation from the French language edition: Femmes et hommes dans le Coran: quelle égalité? by Asma Lamrabet, © Les éditions Albouraq 2012. All Rights Reserved. ISBN 978-2-84161-562-9.

Cover design: Fatima Jamadar

Printed on acid-free paper

This Palgrave Macmillan imprint is published by the registered company Springer International Publishing AG part of Springer Nature
The registered company address is: Gewerbestrasse 11, 6330 Cham, Switzerland

In loving memory of Fatema Mernissi who uncompromisingly but gently pressed me to translate this book. In her words, it was my duty to do so. Now that it's completed, I can see her smiling down on me.

Foreword

While we live in an era in which discussions of Islam—particularly those that proceed outside the Muslim-majority world—tend to be dominated by questions relating to violence, there is no question in my mind that at the heart of the future of this great religious tradition is the question of women. There is no more salient terrain—intellectual, embodied, lived—than this one. It is therefore a great honor to be able to pen a brief foreword for this new edition of Asma Lamrabet's 2012 work *Femmes et hommes dans le Coran: Quelle égalité?*

Thanks to Muneera Salem-Murdock's engaging translation, English-language readers now have access to an important work by one of the foremost public intellectuals writing on Islam and gender today. Lamrabet's work embraces and extends a tradition of scholarship pioneered by a towering figure in the historical sociology of women in Islam, her sister Moroccan the late Fatema Mernissi. Mernissi's work not only revealed the social underpinnings of patriarchal hermeneutics in Islam, it also read back into Islamic history women whose contributions to the construction and articulation of religious authority have been eclipsed by the hegemony of narrative frames inhospitable to the female voice. I always found Mernissi's work so powerful, so persuasive, not only because it shined light on new ways of thinking about women in Islam but also because it also taught us how to identify and critically explore the various ways in which social relations of power are embedded and reflected in any historical process of constructing "orthodoxy."

It is therefore only fitting that Salem-Murdock has dedicated this translation to Fatema's memory.

In *Women and Men in the Qur'ān*, Asma Lamrabet first forces us to confront and then proceeds to dismantle the chimeric "Muslim woman" that animates and assuages a predominantly Euro-American discourse seeking redemption for the Muslim world through her liberation. In a self-described "decolonizing" reading of Islamic sources, she reveals the impossibility of a universalized "Muslim woman" through the diverse experiences of the many women who populate the Qur'ān itself much less the vast and varied cultural geography of the contemporary Muslim world. While making a formidable case for the centrality of the equality of women and men as a Qur'ānic principle of paramount importance, Lamrabet does not shy away from engaging directly with those verses and passages of revelation that seem to establish different and seemingly unequal standards for the two genders. This is a skillful work of contextualized religious hermeneutics that deserves a place alongside other pioneering works such as Amina Wadud's *Qur'ān and Woman* and Asma Barlas' *"Believing Women" in Islam: Unreading Patriarchal Interpretations of the Qur'ān*.

Women and Men in the Qur'ān enables perspectives and dialogue that will be crucial to the production of a conception of gender equality that is as authentic as it is uncompromising—in short, important new directions and hopeful ideas for highly fraught times.

Prof. Peter Mandaville
Ali Vural Ak Center for Global Islamic Studies
George Mason University
Fairfax, USA

CONTENTS

CHAPTER 1

Introduction

It is universally recognized that discrimination against women is an integral part of all cultures and religions. Today, however, only Islam, both as a civilization and as a religion, continues to be mercilessly blasted, put on the defensive, and denounced for what is regarded as its unequal treatment of women, which in turn leads to making the topic of gender inequality central to any discussion of Islam, making it extremely difficult to offer an alternative objective methodology to tackle the question. Moreover, one continues to perceive the issue through a double prism—that of the news media, with its display of stereotypes and widespread Islamophobia, and that of the political ideology of predominantly Muslim societies. This, added to the current transnational political situation, has resulted in Islam being perceived as the religion of the oppression of women par excellence, in total disregard of the significant discrimination vis-à-vis differing societies, traditions, or religions practiced by the accusing cultures.

Persistent discourse and media hype surrounding Muslim women with their precarious legal status, their trailing emancipation, their confining cultural guardianships, and their various *burqas*[1] and "veils" has created, in the contemporary collective imagination, a fixed image of a Muslim woman, eternally submissive and totally overlooked. Such an underhanded image serves to preserve the view that inequality between

---

[1] A *burqa* is an outer garment that covers the entire body from head to toe. It is worn by women when in public in some Islamic countries.

© The Author(s) 2018
A. Lamrabet, *Women and Men in the Qur'ān*,
https://doi.org/10.1007/978-3-319-78741-1_1

the sexes is intrinsic exclusively to the Islamic ideology, thereby removing any need for further analysis or reflection. This in turn creates a relentless determination to liberate and empower these Muslim women who, without exception, suffer from a tyrannical and biased religion, with barbaric overtones. And such liberation can be realized only through idealized Western pathways and led by those prepared to battle in favor of the victims until the bitter end.

This "need" to liberate Muslim women, brought about by a no-longer disguised Western intellectual ethnocentrism, serves to exempt other cultures and societies, especially in the West, from any charges of discrimination against their own women, as if these women were born liberated and in full possession of all of their rights.

This "intellectual" entitlement to meddle, deeply rooted in Western ideology, has virtually become a prerequisite in politically correct rhetoric. *Free the poor Muslim women, victims of Islam* has become a political formula that "sells" and reaffirms the speaker's membership in the "civilized" world, thus further defining the cultural boundaries between Us and Them.

Herein, it would be worth bringing two pieces of evidence to the reader's attention. The first concerns the great diversity among Muslim societies and Muslim women: from Indonesia to Morocco, passing through Saudi Arabia or Central Europe and Sub-Saharan Africa, each of which displays a range of sociocultural heterogeneity and geography. This clear plurality is a blatant contradiction to the constant and unvarying images of Muslim women as projected by Western stereotypes that methodically reduce such women to a single cultural stereotype. The second evidence we tend to overlook is that of the "universality" of a culture of discrimination against women. Unequal rights of women have been the norm for millennia, and despite the undeniable achievements we witness today, women, generally speaking, continue to hold junior positions compared to men, a reality that endures in varying degrees in all cultures and civilizations.

In this postmodern and extremely globalized world of ours, it is the interweaving of patriarchy and ultraliberalism that leads to new forms of exploitation and domination. In the South, as in the North, women find themselves in the same precarious situation. Today, we need to recognize that despite some remarkable progress, equality, this fundamental principle of democratic systems everywhere, remains one of the most unfulfilled promises of the modern world—the struggle for recognition and institutionalization of equal rights for men and women remains incomplete.[2]

That said, the point here is not to reject all criticism of the actual discrimination that Muslim women suffer, particularly when it comes from the West, as some Islamic discourse has done, entirely fixated on the notion of a fantastical Western plot against Islam. What must be rejected is not so much the criticism itself, which may be valid, but the tendency for this criticism to be directed almost uniquely at Islam. This biased criticism, in addition to disregarding the general condition in which most women around the world live, ignores many forms of discrimination, religious, and/or other that women outside the Muslim world are subjected to.

Like other women in the world, Muslim women live subject to the degree of development in their respective societies and their own set of discriminatory rules. Unfortunately, the presence in the mainstream religious arena of a common set of "religious data" and understanding has become the source of cultural discrimination against Muslim women. From where does this "unquestionable" universal image of Islam as a religion that oppresses women, and inevitably hinders their emancipation, originate? It cannot be repeated often enough that it is not Islam as a spiritual message that oppresses women. It is rather the never-reformed legal provisions and interpretations, endorsed for centuries by Muslim scholars (ʿulamā), which have displaced the sacred text and transformed it into inflexible religious laws.

It is very important to distinguish between Islam as a spiritual message and Islam as a culture with its institutions, ideologies, and interpretations. This distinction becomes even more critical when this issue is analyzed, not an easy task in view of the current state of intellectual confusion within Muslim communities and societies. It should also be noted that beyond a Western rhetoric that occasionally borders on indecency, and whose objective might not be as innocent as it may appear, this question of women—especially given what it entails in terms of legal and other rights, such as the equality between men and women—touches

---

[2] Global statistics concerning women are alarming: 100 million missing women in Asia, trafficking of women in the heart of Europe, widespread violence against women everywhere. In her lifetime, at least one woman in three has been beaten, coerced into sex, or otherwise abused, http://www.amnestyusa.org/women.

one of the major problems of Arab-Muslim societies, namely the absence of a genuine democratic space.

The ability to debate and promote the equal rights of women and men in a society is to accept and promote the fundamentals of political democratization. It is this democratic deficiency that is responsible for the failure of a great majority of the reforms undertaken in the Arab-Muslim world, including those concerning the issue of gender equality.

In parody, to a certain extent, of the current situation in Muslim societies regarding gender disparity, we might say that the debate oscillates between two converging discourses. The first is official, a marginally legitimizing policy of "tolerance" that is highlighted by some, usually minor policy actions for the benefit of women, as a symbol of its modernization policy while, at the same time, safeguarding the viability of a rigorous religious interpretation. The other is illustrative of a collective Muslim reality that, in religious debates, makes the "status quo" regarding the issue of women a banner of its cultural resistance to Westernization.[3] In short, in the Muslim world, the concept of equality between men and women continues to be perceived as a Western hegemonic imposition, completely foreign to Islamic tradition. Thus, the issue of women becomes the pole around which all resistance is erected and recurrent frustrations crystallized, which results in it remaining a hostage of a range of interlocking factors, thus making any attempt at understanding it, let alone finding resolutions, problematic.

Accordingly, the subject of Muslim women and their rights has been and remains a hostage of an anticolonial struggle and its postmodern geopolitical consequences (Palestine; Iraq; Afghanistan; September 11). These conflicts serve to invigorate identity crises in the Muslim world and delegitimize any attempt at reform, particularly on the issue of Muslim women, who are regarded as the guardians of the last Islamic bastion and hence in need of protection.

The issue of women and equality in Islam can be understood only by seeing through multiples lenses—from the central point of view of

---

[3] Take the example of the family code in Morocco. Since the prerequisite educational and religious reforms upstream were not carried out in advance, while the family code has certainly been a legal breakthrough, it has not yet been ingrained in the minds of people whose poor understanding of the importance of justice and equality within the family has basically remained unchanged.

political governance in the majority of Arab-Islamic autocracies to the unending problem of endless updating (*aggiornamento*) and reform of Islamic tradition and thought—while passing through the problems of economic and technical underdevelopment. Because the question is multifaceted, solutions to offer can only derive from a pluralistic and consensual reflection that takes into account all of these factors.

This book in no way pretends to address all of these concerns. Rather, it is an attempt to decipher and discern the meaning of some Qur'ānic references that favor equality between men and women. This is done by tracing the origin of religious disputes while attempting to deconstruct—as much as possible—the countless interpretations and erroneous ideas that surround these references. Thus, this contemporary analysis of the interpretations of the Qur'ān is primarily a modest contribution to the ongoing debate of equality between men and women in Islam. It should be noted that while referring essentially to the Qur'ān, and to a lesser degree, to the *hadīth* (the sayings and doings of the Prophet Mohamed),[4] this analysis never loses sight of the relevant sociopolitical and cultural conditions of this time of history. It is simply a matter of returning to the basics of the spiritual message of Islam concerning human relationships and to reflect on the countless passages that emphasize the importance of shared responsibility, mutual support, and respect between a man and a woman. And it is an exercise of reflecting on the relational ethics between men and women as conceived by the scriptural sources of Islam in which the reader is invited to partake.

Values, so simple, so beautiful, reiterated in this profound Qur'ānic language that, unfortunately, the hearts have not retained, and tightly sealed mentalities have ousted and relegated to the recesses of history. Human values, truly universal, are sorely lacking in our present daily lives—lives that have sadly been turned upside down by the turmoil of muddled modernity and the loss of crucial points of reference.

---

[4]The prophetic tradition—*Sunnah*—is the implementation of the Qur'ānic ethics, as symbolized by the sayings and doings of Prophet Muhammad. It is historically proven that the Prophet was one of the principal defenders of women's rights who strived to implement them on the grounds of reality. Recounting the entire prophetic tradition (*Hadīth*) on this topic would require a separate book; however, examples are cited throughout this study in support of the intentions of the various Qur'ānic views.

PART I

Women in Islam: A New Approach

CHAPTER 2

Beyond the Problematic of "The Muslim Woman"

Before proceeding further in our discussion, it would be useful to clarify a conceptual blunder that, at first glance, may seem unimportant, but is in fact indicative of the shallowness of the debates regarding different issues related to women in Islam. These issues are often analyzed in categorical terms that encapsulate the totality of the problems encountered by Muslim women everywhere, within a single designation—*the Muslim Woman*. Here, the question that begs an answer is, which Muslim woman are we talking about? The Asian or the African? The North African or the Middle Easterner? The Muslim women of the Gulf or those from Balkan states? Western Europeans or North Americans? Residents of Dubai or those living in the Egyptian countryside? The Bengali Muslim woman who lives like a slave in the palaces of Riyadh, or the young Turkish woman living in the suburbs of Istanbul?

It is true that one may easily identify a common denominator for all these women that of religion—Islam—which has become associated with a set of rules and regulations, often derived from misogynistic interpretations, justified in the name of religion. But even there, the manner in which such culture of discrimination in the name of religion manifests itself is very diverse depending on the geopolitical and sociocultural environments of these women, their academic and economic backgrounds, and their ability to battle for their rights. So, residing in very different environments, Muslim women cannot but interact differently with the oppressive discriminatory rules and regulations under which they live

© The Author(s) 2018
A. Lamrabet, *Women and Men in the Qur'ān*,
https://doi.org/10.1007/978-3-319-78741-1_2

and operate. Reducing such diversity of contexts and reactions to a single rigidly defined entity—the Muslim Woman—is absurd.

Historically speaking, it is important to remember that this designation of "the Muslim Woman" is quite recent. Indeed, ever since the late nineteenth century Arab Renaissance (*Nahda*), a women-focused Islamic discourse tends to trap these women into slogans of "rights and responsibilities of Women in Islam" or "the status of women in Islam"; despite the good intentions that lie beneath, such designations are doubly demoting because they tend, as mentioned earlier, to overshadow the great diversity of Muslim women in terms of their origins, culture, economic, and social status, and way of life and reduce them to an abstract profile—the Muslim Woman. In addition, by referring to Muslim women as such we reduce the history of all women across this civilization to a single abstract, a supposedly representative profile that is completely inadequate and intellectually and conceptually barren. Reducing all Muslim women to a "Woman" of any kind also overlooks the fact that the Qur'ānic text itself speaks of "Women" in the plural, thus forcefully emphasizing their diversity, as we see in the fourth *sūrah* of the Qur'ān entitled "Women" (*an-nisā'*), not "Woman."

The profiles of women presented by the Qur'ān are as multiple as they are different. Bilqīs, Maryam, and Zoulaïkha,[1] among others, embody, each in her own way, a particular profile of a woman, with its own path and its own trajectory, both sociohistorical and spiritual. Bilqīs is presented as a model of a wise and gifted political ruler, whereas Maryam symbolizes exemplary spiritual excellence and Zoulaïkha perpetual repentance.[2]

Noteworthy is the current discourse in the Muslim arena regarding women's rights in Islam, which has become a mirror image of the international, stereotypical portrait of a victimized Muslim woman without the slightest attention to the broad multidimensional differentiation

---

[1] **Bilqīs**, the tenth century B.C. Queen of Sheba, ruled over a large kingdom that covered the area presently occupied by the countries of Ethiopia, Somalia, and Yemen. Accounts of her wisdom, great wealth, and power and her encounter with King Solomon are related in the holy books of Islam, Christianity, and Judaism and in history books. **Maryam** is a reference to the Virgin Mary. **Zoulaïkha** refers to the woman who tried to seduce Joseph; she was the wife of the chief of the guard in Pharaoh's palace, called Potiphar in the Book of Genesis and Aziz in the Qur'ān.

[2] For more details, on the Qur'ānic profiles of feminine personalities please refer to Asma Lamrabet's book, *Le coran et les femmes: une lecture de libération* (Tawhid, 2007).

that exists in the Muslim world. And the discourse on women's rights in Islam is simplistic because it systematically forces them into particular frames of reference—rights, duties, and status. This selective approach, even if it corresponded to certain realities, has shown its limitations and inadequacies.

Moreover, sorting women into individual "registers" may give the impression that women's rights and status are both "particular" and "discrete" and hence completely different from those of men. It is true that there are some specific verses in the Qur'ān that refer specifically to women, but these should be viewed in their special contexts, as is also the case regarding references to men as men, husbands, or fathers. It should also be realized that this type of Qur'ānic verse is limited and that most messages are addressed to all of humanity, thus transcending any notion of gender, let alone race, ethnic origin, or social class.

There is an explicit Islamic discourse that categorizes women in a monolithic framework, that of the "status or rights of women," when it does not do the same with the masculine equivalent, or makes a specific reference to the "status or rights of men." This inevitably forces the idea of an "Islamic standard," that is of an "ideal man" who represents "human nature" or the "human being" in all of its totality and glory. Following this logic, the woman, in comparison, brings to mind only the image of a structurally subordinate, deficient, dependent, and eternally stigmatized being, given its inability to achieve the universal standard embodied by man.

To speak of women's rights is to decide once and for all that women have the rights that are completely different from those granted to men, inalienable rights that are not subject to debate. It is important to note that in traditional Islamic scholarly work women are never categorized in such a way; neither does one find anything of the sort in the language of traditional legal textbooks concerning women's rights or the status of women in Islam. In all traditional legal structures, women's rights are mentioned only in the chapters on domestic jurisdiction, marriage (*nikāh*), divorce (*talāq*), or provisions concerning both spouses, in other words, the matrimonial sphere.[3]

---

[3] See classic books on Muslim jurisprudence such as *Bidāyat al-mujtahid wa nihāyat al-muqtasid* (*the distinguished jurist's primer*) by Ibn Rushd, translated by Imran Khan Nyazee (Garnet Publishing, 1999) and *Al-fiqh 'ala al-madhāhib al-arba'ah* (*Islamic jurisprudence according to the four sunni schools*) by Abd al-Rahmān al-Jaziri (Fons Vitae, 2009).

To repeat, this particular interpretation—the rights and status of women in Islam—was born within a specific framework, that of the late nineteenth century early Muslim reformers. The initial aim was not only to thwart the liberation model of women as the colonizer conveyed it but also to put forward a new discourse given the deterioration of the status of women in the Arab-Muslim societies of the time. With time, this kind of representation ended by marginalizing the universality of the spiritual message of Islam, which offers a completely different vision, one that affirms the spiritual and human equality of men and women. Indeed, in the Qur'ān, we see the notion of a "human being" (*insān*) or "children of Adam" (*Banī Ādam*) to be, in the unanimous opinion of religious scholars (*'ulamā*), expressions that encompass men and women without distinction.

Thus, by forcing women into rigid grids, we have inadvertently discarded the splendid universal Qur'ānic message and its cosmic vision of the human being, man and woman. It would be only through a return to the original framework, the universality of the Qur'ānic message, that we will be able to overcome these restrictive notions of women's rights or the status of women and to understand, in depth, the universal and particular contribution of Islam to women and men, in all their humanity.

CHAPTER 3

The Qur'ānic Revelation in Seventh-Century Arabia

When we consider the existence or nonexistence of equality between men and women in Islam, we too often eye the Qur'ānic provisions on the subject through the lenses of modern standards of equality and are guided by available information on modern rules and regulations. Such an approach ignores the fact that while the text of the Qur'ān remains very relevant to the current lives of over one-and-a-half billion people, the Qur'ānic text was revealed within a given historical structure, that of seventh-century Arabia. It is in light of such particular context, with its prevailing socioeconomic and sociocultural practices and conditions, that the Qur'ānic revelation regarding equality should be considered, especially given that the concept of equality itself is an evolving notion that cannot be measured independently of the social standards and values of a given time. Equality as understood in the twenty-first century is the product of a profound sociopolitical metamorphosis; the achievements of today would have been absolutely unimaginable a century ago. This is why, to be able to adequately understand equality in the Qur'ān, it is essential to understand the period of its revelation. In fact, by the social and policy standards of that time, certain Qur'ānic provisions are considered entirely pioneering.

It is also of vital importance to differentiate between the revealed corpus—all the provisions and fundamental principles of the holy text—and the various interpretations of that text. The initial momentum and spirit of the Qur'ān, present in all of its prescriptions, reveals a clear empowerment of women and a disposition for establishing egalitarian spirituality.

© The Author(s) 2018
A. Lamrabet, *Women and Men in the Qur'ān*,
https://doi.org/10.1007/978-3-319-78741-1_3

This, however, is not clearly reflected in all of the Islamic interpretations. And if there are some so-called "Islamic" provisions that appear unambiguously discriminatory, they are in fact the product of human interpretations of the revealed texts, interpretations that have meaningfully marked the historical memory of Islam.

The revelation of the Qur'ān remains tied to circumstantial events inherent in the Arabian society of the seventh century. Therefore, one should always grasp the need for a double reading in order to distinguish the spirit of the text, still valid fourteen centuries later, and the response provided by the Qur'ān to an event rooted in the reality of its time. It is very important therefore to assimilate the particular context in order to appreciate the vital contribution of the Islamic revelation in this original environment and to value the incredible timelessness of the message, everlastingly rejuvenating in the hearts of its believers, worldwide. Indeed, even a brief look at the historical journey of this religion would allow us not only to recognize the importance of the provisions proposed by the Qur'ān for both women and men but also to measure the distance that separates the Qur'ān's spiritual message from subsequent flawed interpretations.

The proliferation of interpretative readings with discriminatory leanings has subsequently, and in a short span of time, forced aside the fundamental equality of the spiritual content of the message while preserving the strong undertones of the traditional sexual hierarchy of the society.

Most contemporary historians describe the Qur'ānic revelation as an event that caused an upheaval on three levels: (1) transcendental (the restoration of *tawhīd* or the affirmation of the principle of the oneness of the Creator in which both the male and female believers[1] overcome all alienation, whether material or moral); (2) political, in the sense of a new concept of governance, based on sociopolitical egalitarianism; and (3) the rehabilitation of the social status of the women of the time and a reorientation of relations between men and women toward greater equality and interactive participation.

---

[1] It should be noted that, whether in reference to animate or inanimate objects, singular or plural, nouns in Arabic must indicate gender (feminine or masculine), with the masculine form being the default. For example, *ustādh* is a male teacher, whereas *ustādhah* is a female teacher; likewise, *mumarridh* is a male nurse, whereas *mumarridhah* is a female nurse.

The year 610 marks the "Islam Event," the revelation of the first verse of the Qur'ān to Prophet Muhammad. We should remember that this revelation was none other than an unprecedented call for "Knowledge" announced in the formal injunction *Iqra'*, *Read!* Read the Revelation Book as well as the Book of the Universe and Creation. "Read," the first word of the Qur'ān, embodies the importance given to adjudication, to awareness, and to the pursuit of knowledge (*'ilm*). *Iqra'* is the Qur'ānic incitement to awaken the senses, to awaken human curiosity regarding the sacred and the world, the awareness of the voice of God in every human being.

Islam, as the Qur'ān reminds us in several passages, is not a new religion; it is the culmination of other monotheist revelations commenced by the Prophet Abraham,[2] a new dimension of the monotheistic approach that, with the Qur'ānic revelation, reaches its zenith, its ultimate consecration, and its final recognition. The notion of *dhikr* (remembrance) is repeatedly reiterated in the Qur'ān as a reminder to all mankind to venerate God, the one and only.[3]

As an extension of other monotheistic traditions—Judaism and Christianity—Islam is the expression of the *dhikr* of the divine word, a word that, while coming from the same source, transcends time and space, the "Supreme Book" (*umm-al-kitāb*), mentioned in the Qur'ān. It is in this sense that, at the advent of Islam, earlier religions are referred to as "religions of the Book" because they all emanate from the same celestial Book, the science reserved to God alone, and He alone is the All Knowledgeable.[4]

[2]Abraham is venerated by Islam and Muslims and is referenced numerous times in the Qur'ān. The Qur'ān relates how he preached to his community, including his father, whom the Qur'ān calls Azar, reproaching them for taking idols for gods and urging them to abandon such idols in favor of the One God (Qur'ān 6:74; 19:41–50; 21:51–73; 26:86–89; 29:16–28; 37:83–89; 43:26–28). The Qur'ān also describes Abraham as a *Hanīf*, the Pure or the Upright (2:35; 3:67; 4:125) and as a friend of God, *Khalil-Allah* (4:125).

[3]"It is naught but a reminder for the worlds" (Qur'ān 81:27; 12:104; 38:87; 68:52). Unless otherwise specified, the English translations of this verse and others throughout this book follow Nasr et al., *The Study Qur'ān: A New Translation and Commentary* (HarperOne, 2015).

[4]*Tafsīr Ibn 'Ashūr, At-tahrīr wa at-tanwīr*. Dar Ihya' Al Turāth, 2000. Commentary on verse 39 of *sūrah* 13: *Umm al-kitāb* is the knowledge (*'ilm*) of God that only He knows. *Tafsīr*, also known as Qur'ānic Commentaries, is a body of commentary and clarification notes, aimed at explaining the meanings of the Qur'ān. Generally speaking, there are three categories of *Tafsīr*: Classical Arabic, Modern Arabic, and *Tafsīr* in other languages.

Abraham, Moses, and Jesus are cited in the Qur'ān as among the great prophets who transmitted the divine message at different stages of the history of humanity. Repeatedly altered, the message has been transmitted again through a succession of messengers, with Muhammad representing, along the same line, the last of the envoys, bearer of the Holy Qur'ān, the ultimate spiritual message.

However, this vision of the other monotheistic religions is neither downgrading nor exclusionary in the sense that these other spiritual traditions would now be null and void. On the contrary, they remain living sources that mark the infinity of pathways to God and His eternal Spring. The Qur'ān is unambiguous on the subject, advocating a reciprocal acceptance of all spiritual pathways, as we see in the following verse:

> And We have sent down unto thee the Book in truth, confirming the Book that came before it, and as a protector over it. So judge between them in accordance with what God has sent down, and follow not their caprices away from the truth that has come unto thee. For each among you We have appointed a law and a way. And had God willed, He would have made you one community, but [He willed otherwise], that He might try you in that which He has given you. So vie one with another in good deeds. Unto God shall be your return all together, and He will inform you of that wherein you differ.[5]

The terms "Islam" and "Muslim" are perceived today in a most restricted fashion: a religion that is limited to specific populations designated as Muslims by their culture and geography as well as their religion. However, Islam is above all a "spiritual disposition" that considers a Muslim as anyone who engages willingly and consciously in the recognition of God as the One Creator of this world. In this regard, the Qur'ān stresses that all the prophets before Muhammad were "Muslim" in the sense that they had "a consciousness of God and His Creation." The notion of "Muslim"[6] in the Qur'ān thus notes that "original belief,"

---

[5] The Qur'ān 5:48.

[6] Most Arabic words are derived from three-consonant "roots" that embody the meaning or meanings of a word. For example, the root of the words *kataba* (he wrote), *kitāb* (a book), *kātib* (a male author, writer, or clerk), or *kātibah* (a female author, writer, or clerk) is *k-t-b*, from which the words above and many other words that tend to be related are derived. Muslim and Islam are derived from the root *s, l, m, Salama*, which signifies submission, in this case to the will of the One and Only God. Thus, in a general sense, all monotheists are by definition Muslims in the sense that they are in total surrender to the One God, no matter the pathway such surrender might follow.

called *fitrah*, a fundamental concept in Islam, a concept that boils down to the very essence of Qur'ānic spirituality. *Fitrah*, in this sense, is nothing other than this "innate predisposition" toward faith in God, a disposition that is most frequently consigned to the human unconscious.

This Qur'ānic vision of faith and the definition of Islam and "how to be a Muslim" are actually understood only via an ethnic-cultural dimension, a dimension that today appears to have lost its universal "aura" but which, at some point in the history of this civilization, has created some of the best scholars and scholarships known to humankind.[7]

The advent of Islam in Arabia was not fortuitous. A commercial, cultural, and religious crossroad, Mecca was the ideal breeding ground for hatching a new expression of monotheistic spirituality. One often depicts the pre-Islamic period in Arabia (*al-Jāhiliyya*) as a dark and barbaric period. This image is warranted in relation to certain customs. Nevertheless, we must recognize other rewarding aspects of that time, even if it is due only to the intensity of trade, economic, and cultural crossbreeding that the Arabian Peninsula experienced at the time. Such positive attributes would include the spirit of chivalry, the sense of honor, a very rich oral tradition, the remembrance of genealogies, and above all, Arabic poetry, which was one of the most thriving arts in the cultural life of the period. Judaism and Christianity were also, and for a long time, present in the Arabian Peninsula, as well as other forms of religious syncretism, especially among Meccan tribes, who were the most hostile to the Qur'ānic message.

In fact, the Arabian Peninsula was governed by a clan order in which the authority of trade, the strength of ethnic origin or clan spirit (*'asabiyyah qabaliyyah*), and tribal warfare were the only recognized governing social standards. Islam would upstage this order not only spiritually and culturally but also and primarily at the level of the demand for justice, thereby challenging the despotic and unequal tribal system that reigned at the time. The *jāhiliyyah* also corresponds, according to the Qur'ānic revelation, to a period of "ignorance of God." The Qur'ān often speaks pejoratively of certain customs of this period because, most often, they were considered contrary to reason. Some polytheists of the *Quraysh* tribe worshiped the true God of Abraham but with the intermediacy of

---

[7]The reference is to philosophers and scholars who lived during the golden age of the Judeo-Islamic culture such as Avicenna, Averroes, and Maimonides.

a multitude of deities at the *Ka'ba*,[8] not to mention, as an aside, the fact that these idols proved to be very profitable for Mecca notables.

It is not a question for the new revelation to undermine a culture in its entirety or to weaken pre-established traditions as a whole; rather, the aim is to reinvigorate and restore certain ethical standards of morality and social behavior. Did not the Prophet of Islam himself affirm, "I was sent to complete the beautiful mores,"[9] which confirms the pre-existence of a universal moral code that Islam did not intend to annul; neither did it intend to reserve cultural exclusivity for itself. The spiritual message was revealed at that time in history to restore, improve, and perpetuate this universal morality.

So, while certain barbaric customs will be completely abolished, others will be preserved and some others will be subjected to profound transformations, while maintaining the dominant cultural framework. An example among many others is that of the pilgrimage to Mecca (*hajj*) and the circumambulation around the *Ka'ba*, which was a part of pre-Islamic religious ritual. The idols of the *Ka'ba* were in fact glorified and worshiped by all of the Arab tribes who, each year, observed this religious rite in the name of a polytheistic reading of the Abrahamic tradition. Islam will radically modify the spirit of this ritual while maintaining its form and cultural framework. Ali Shariati, a prominent Iranian scholar, rightly refers to this as "an internal revolution against traditions together with the maintenance of their positive forms" (my translation).[10]

The key point to remember about this spiritual upheaval is the fact that the society of that period shall realize "liberation" from oppression. The Qur'ānic message is particularly uncompromising when it comes to the fight against all forms of social subordination and the demand for justice and liberation. These two concepts of Justice (*al-'adl*) and

---

[8] *Ka'ba* is the holiest structure in Islam, located in the town of Mecca, Saudi Arabia. It is also the *qibla*, the direction that Muslims turn to when they pray.

[9] A *hadīth* reported by Abou Hurayra in *Sahīh al-Bukhari*, no. 273. *Sahīh al-Bukhāri* is a collection of *hadīths* compiled by Imam Muhammad al-Bukhari (d. 870), recognized by the overwhelming majority of the Muslim world to be the most authentic collection of reports of *the Sunnah of the Prophet Muhammad*. The collection is composed of over 7500 *hadīths* (with some repetition) in 97 books. The translation was done by Dr. M. Muhsin Khan.

[10] Ali Shariati, *Fatima est Fatima, l'idéal universel feminine* (Albouraq, 2009).

liberation or the plight of the downtrodden on earth (*al-mustad'ifoun fil-ard*) are at the heart of the spiritual message, as corroborated by many Qur'ānic verses, that only by being free can the human being become conscious of and worship God in His plenitude, in other words, serve and be useful to others. There is no greater act of worship than the constant quest to be of utility to and in solidarity with others, which is a manner of achieving one's humanity. In this sense, the Prophet said, "The best of you is he who shows to be the best and most useful to others!"[11] This *hadīth* confirms the fact that a commitment to the defense of human rights—to use the modern jargon—is a commitment to the Creation of God and therefore a commitment to God.

The first companions of the Prophet well understood this requirement to defend the right of others and to administer justice, and they all tried to do so, each in his way. The second caliph 'Umar Ibn al-Khatāb asserts this value in Egypt, confronted by the arrogant attitude of one of his governors ('Amr ibn al-'As), whose son had deliberately assaulted a Copt: "By what right do you oppress a human being whose mother brought into this world free?"[12] And Imām 'Ali who frequently offered his close entourage the advice: "Don't be a slave to another when God created you free!"[13] The new Qur'ānic message has thus arrived in order profoundly to transform the ethical values that reigned in the area and throughout the world to surmount the narrow clannish spirit and sway it toward the force of reason, to challenge injustice that is instigated by the feudal viewpoint of social justice, and to replace the reign of servitude by that of freedom of conscience and of choice.

Reason, freedom, and a sense of justice are the fundamental values at the heart of the Qur'ānic faith that Islam came to rekindle from the ashes of the oblivion where earlier messages were buried, the ashes of indifference that had seized the hearts of mankind.

---

[11] Al-Suyūti, *Al-jāmi' As-saghīr*, *hadīth*, no. 4044. Imam Jalaluddin al-Suyuti (1445–1505) was an Egyptian scholar, jurist, and prolific writer.

[12] 'Ali Tāntawi and Nāji Tāntawi, *Akhbār 'Umar wa akhbar 'Abdillah ibn 'Umar*, 8th edition (Beirut, 1983), p. 145.

[13] *Nahj al-blāgha*, letter no. 31, Part 3, p. 52. *Nahj al-blāgha* (*Peak of Eloquence*) is a compilation of 'Ali ibn Abu Tālib's sermons, letters, and sayings, by Sayyid al-Sharif ar-Rādi, more than 1000 years ago. The Shia Muslims consider it to be the most valuable book after the Qur'ān.

It is through this fundamental value of the Qur'ānic faith that the issue of gender equality, intrinsic to the spiritual message of Islam, could and should be understood. It is through these three fundamental values of Islam that we should reread the Qur'ān and exchange the theme of women and men for that of the liberation of human beings, be they men or women.

CHAPTER 4

An Alternative Approach to the Qur'ān

The current prevailing ideological confusion in debates on Islam, especially around the notion of equality, is directly related to the conventional approach used to study the religious text and to the fragmentation of religious knowledge. Rather than thinking of the Qur'ān holistically, the Sacred Text is fragmented in order to draw short-range solutions for increasingly profound societal ills. But the ethical values transmitted by the Qur'ān cannot be fully understood unless they are captured in their entirety, with due respect accorded to the internal cohesion of the text, and all the ideals that constitute its foundation.

A deeper understanding of the question of women in Islam and its corollary, equality, requires a new holistic and didactic approach to the original source. It is no longer sufficient to be satisfied with the extraction of Qur'ānic verses that deal with women, as has always been the case, to date. Rather, it is a matter of putting the particular verses back into their Qur'ānic normative framework, which corresponds to a global vision of humanity for both men and women. In other words, we need to understand what the Qur'ān says about women as well as about men, and such understanding should come from within the relational framework pertaining to the holistic vision of the Qur'ān.

To achieve this, it would be useful to distinguish, from within the holistic framework, three levels of readings of Qur'ānic verses: (1) those of universal scope, which constitute the majority of verses; (2) situational verses, which are linked to a historical incident; and (3) specific verses, which are revealed for women or for men, or for specific women and specific men.

© The Author(s) 2018
A. Lamrabet, *Women and Men in the Qur'ān*,
https://doi.org/10.1007/978-3-319-78741-1_4

Verses of Universal Scope

Verses of universal scope constitute the major part of the Qur'ān and are addressed, without distinction, to both men and women. These verses encompass a set of norms, values, and key principles that form the foundation of behavioral ethics for women and men in Islam. Values such as justice, equality, and excellence (*ihsān*) are used as the benchmarks that permit the evaluation of the personal engagement of men and women in spiritual piety (*at-taqwā*). These key concepts of equality, universal in their formulation and in their purpose, constitute a natural vehicle for the spiritual message of Islam; a true understanding and appreciation of Qur'ānic philosophy and wisdom (*hikmah*) can only by attained through a comprehensive interpretation and deep understanding of these concepts. It is in this fashion that the spiritual message of Islam in its global perspective transmits a set of universal values found in the egalitarian vision of the creation of men and women, in the egalitarian enlightenment of human civilization, in principles such as moral integrity, in the ethics of the marital union, in the co-responsibility of men and women, and in many other precepts, detailed in the pages that follow.

Situational Verses

Situational verses are those that remain linked to a given spatiotemporal framework, namely that of the Arab society of the seventh century. Thus, these verses try to respond to the sociocultural imperatives of an era while, at the same time, gently attempt to instill the deep societal transformations that Islam had founded. Examples of such verses abound, including those that speak of slavery, war-related plunders (booty), concubinage, and corporal punishment.

Regarding slavery, while Islam has certainly not abolished it, the Qur'ān strongly emphasizes the importance of the emancipation of slaves and considers it to be an act of piety and wisdom. This emphasis formed part of the progressive dimension of Qur'ānic education, whose goal was to introduce substantive reforms while focusing on the gradual transformation of attitudes and understandings. The liberation of slaves (*tahrīr raqaba*) was thus a temporary measure of atonement, a way of "mending" a large number of crimes and blunders and a pathway toward the gradual establishment of a new consciousness, one that is respectful of human dignity and liberty.

Thus, numerous Qur'ānic verses motivate believers to free slaves and to restore their legal status through marriage and the protection of their rights.[1] It remains true, however, that despite the insistent encouragement of the Qur'ān to liberate slaves, it did not insist on its abolition because slavery as a practice had long persisted among the Arabs, and Arab-Muslim societies were not ready for its total eradication.

In reference to slavery, we must keep in mind that in its various forms and since antiquity it has been a norm that no society appeared prepared to relinquish. The history of the slave trade from Africa had its dreadful peak with the colonization of the New World, and slavery in the West has allowed the development of equally shameful ideologies of racism and white supremacy whose last stronghold was the apartheid regime in South Africa in the twentieth century. The abolition of slavery at the international level has also progressed in stages, beginning in the late eighteenth and early nineteenth centuries. However, slavery was not truly abolished until after World War II. Throughout the world, the last two nations to have formally abolished slavery are Muslim, namely Saudi Arabia in 1962 and Mauritania in 1980.[2]

Regarding harems and concubinage, it was during the Umayyad period that these disgraceful institutions were introduced and readily accepted by the society, with the status of concubines being reserved for female slaves. And the harem became an institution that, for centuries, took Muslim women as hostages and condemned them to virtual silence and for many to intellectual and political anguish. The harem and its concubines with its fantasized exotic oriental images that personify "Muslim-Arab" misogyny will for a long-time fuel the Western imagination and remain a reflection of a stereotypical image of a certain Islam.

Both the spoils of war and concubinage enter into the same registry as slavery. The Qur'ān speaks of all three as observed, without taking sides, while at the same time introducing measures aimed at the eventual dismissal of these archaic traditions without undermining the foundations of the society of the time, as a whole.

---

[1] The Qur'ān 4:92; 2:177; 90:12; 58:3; 5:89.

[2] "L'Antiquité à nos jours: L'esclavage, une realité qui dure," https://www.herodote.net/De_l_Antiquite_a_nos_jours-synthese-16.ph.

The Specific Verses

The specific verses are those linked to a particular conjuncture of events that remain important in terms of their general application and objective, especially the sense of justice that underpins them. Some of the verses that pertain specifically to women might appear archaic or even discriminatory when viewed in reference to modern values. However, it is necessary to distinguish the final objective of these verses from the language in which they were revealed and to place the focus on the purpose of the message rather than on the letter of the text.

Thus, certain verses such as those that evoke polygamy, inheritance rules among siblings, individual testimony, or the verse in which we see an uncorroborated permission to "strike" the wife[3] summarize the basics of Islam as viewed by many Muslim and non-Muslim scholars. And it is this vision that has contributed to the bad reputation of this religion.

Taking these verses out of the normative egalitarian framework of the Qur'ānic vision, then submitting them to shockingly discriminatory word-for-word readings and interpretations has resulted in the creation and preservation of the pejorative vision of a religion that oppresses women, and where notions of equality are virtually absent. In fact, these verses can be understood only by starting with Qur'ānic history, the very moment of the supreme Revelation, and the sociocultural upheavals born of that original transcendental eruption. As a matter of fact, during the twenty-three years of Revelation, the Qur'ān has instated a genuine social transformation relative to the status that was reserved for women. The social advances that were realized are comparable to or surpass that attained by the great civilizations of that time period.

It is astonishing that of the **6236** Qur'ānic verses, and despite the importance of women's role in the Qur'ānic global vision and the social transformations generated by this vision, most readings of the Qur'ān have focused on a few specific verses, four or five, thus ultimately

---

[3] The expression *wa-dribūhunna* in the said verse comes from the root **d**, **r**, **b**, *daraba*, which has about thirty meanings such as "walk" (*daraba fil-ard*) and "giving as an example" (*daraba Mathalan*). In verse 34 of *sūrah* 4, the expression is interpreted literally and classically in the sense of "*strike them.*" In fact, this interpretation has been called into question by a number of contemporary scholars who prefer substituting it for "stay away from them," which better corresponds with the Qur'ānic objectives. For more details, see *Le Coran et les femmes, une lecture de libération* and the detailed analyses by Dr. Al-'Ajami, https://oumma.com/frapper-sa-femme-avec-le-coran-12/.

reducing the entire spiritual message to the scale of the interpretations of the said verses.

In this chapter, we will deal in a succinct fashion with only one example—polygamy. Other examples, such as inheritance, the presumed authority of men over women, testimony, and others will be analyzed in more depth, in the following chapters.

POLYGAMY

The verse that speaks about polygamy is an example of what we identified earlier as *Specific Verses*, which accompanied the transformation of the social mores of Arabia at the moment of the Qur'ānic revelation. Taken out of its Qur'ānic context and considering it in isolation, polygamy becomes a determining element in caricaturing Islam. "*Islam permits polygamy*" has become one of the favorite denunciations and customary clichés, mindlessly uttered by many for whom Islam is the religion of the Other, in total disregard for the fact that Islam did not invent polygamy, a system practiced by virtually all civilizations, during a certain period of history. In the Arab-Islamic world, while most men might have aspired to have several wives, polygamy was practiced by only a minority, rarely exceeding 5% of marriages.[4] In Africa, polygamy constitutes an important element of societal norms, with 30–55% of women living within polygamous households. In short, widespread polygamy has nothing to do with Islam, as has been shown in a number of studies. Among traditional animists, polygamy constitutes about 47.5% of marriages, a level that is much higher than what we see among Muslims. And in certain regions of Africa, especially in Chad, one finds a higher rate of polygamy among Catholics than among Muslims living in the same regions.[5]

Qur'ānic verses that speak about polygamy should be considered in their context of pre-Islamic Arabia, where the number of wives a man could have was unlimited, and where having several wives was a deep-rooted ancestral tradition and a symbol of affluence. In the Qur'ān, the verse that speaks of polygamy is part and parcel of a set of recommendations concerning widows and orphans, especially widows with

---

[4] Youssef Courbage and Emmanuel Todd, *Le rendez-vous des civilisations, La République des idées*. France: Seuil, 2007, p. 60.

[5] Ibid., p. 61.

orphaned children who, during the pre-Islamic period, were sought out for marriage by men whose primary motivation was the confiscation of their inheritance:

> Give orphans their property, and exchange not the bad for the good, nor consume their property with your own. Truly that would be a great sin. If you fear that you will not deal fairly with the orphans, then marry such women as seem good to you, two, three, or four; but if you fear that you will not deal justly, then only one, or those whom your right hands possess. Thus it is more likely that you will not commit injustice.[6]

As made very clear in the verse, the primary goal is the protection of orphans by swaying men away from this repulsive custom, marrying the mothers in order to control their wealth, by means of limiting the number of wives to four. As such, it is not a matter of an everlasting legislative verse, but of a permission given in order to address a compelling social problem.

In a second phase, the permission is conditioned by a limitation that was aimed at reducing the probability of polygamous marriages: fairness to orphans and strict equality among the spouses: "but if you fear that you will not deal justly, then only one." Indeed, fear of inequity effectively prohibits polygamy (for those who choose to follow Qur'ānic directives), as equity among wives is unachievable; polygamy is therefore very unlikely to occur, if we want to respect the Qur'ānic obligation.

It is in a third phase that the Qur'ān announces its clear disapproval of polygamy, in a verse that explicitly demonstrates the effective impossibility of being fair and equitable in the context of a polygamous marriage: "You will not be able to deal fairly between women, even if it is your ardent desire."[7] One should consider this last verse as an endorsement of monogamy because it alone can ensure fairness, good balance, and marital stability.

Unfortunately, in the history of Islam, many interpretations of the Qur'ān resulted in making the first "permission" the **rule**, at the expense of the verse recommending monogamy as the norm in marriage in Islam. The "deterrence" expressed by the Qur'ān and the clear recommendation of monogamy were surpassed by the reality of polygamy being

---

[6] The Qur'ān 4:2–3.
[7] The Qur'ān 4:129.

strongly anchored in Bedouin tribal culture, but also through Islamic law (*Fiqh*) that will make polygamy one of the principles that demonstrate the superiority and dominance of men over women. Indeed, polygamy, though disapproved by the Qur'ān, was extracted from its Qur'ānic framework by some Muslim jurists (*fuqahā'*) of the classic era and reinstated it, in the name of religion, into the local customs as a criterion of superiority of men to women.

The jurists have interpreted the earlier verses on polygamy as a kind of *carte blanche* to have multiple partners, and appended such "permission" to the registry of sexual benefits allowed to men. As we have seen, given the patriarchal tribal society of Arabia, the primary intent of these verses was the protection of the most vulnerable minorities of the time, women, widows, and orphans, and has absolutely nothing to do with the sexuality of men. Finally, let us take note of Muslim reformers of the Arab Renaissance era, such as Imām Muhammad 'Abduh in Egypt and some of his contemporaries such as the Moroccan scholar Allal el-Fassi; neither of the two has hesitated in calling for the outright ban of polygamy in their respective countries.[8]

THE OTHER APPROACH TO THE QUR'ĀN: THE HOLISTIC APPROACH

The Islamic principle that the Qur'ān is a valid text, applicable to any time and any place, is intrinsically linked to the ability of believers to differentiate among the various levels of Qur'ānic representations, in complete harmony with their devotion, in terms of both the ethics of the spiritual message and the contingent realities of the era in which they live. Such devotion therefore requires a distinction between these different reading registers, the temporal and the universal, i.e. between universal and inviolable principles, on the one hand, and the particular and the contingent, on the other. So, it is by making this distinction between general key concepts, specific verses, and situational verses that it becomes easier to understand the global vision of the Qur'ān, including the specific guidelines for men and women.

Viewing the question of women and men holistically, within the framework of this trajectory, would entail a return to the Qur'ānic vision

---

[8] Allal El-Fassi, *An-naqd adh-dhati* (Self-Criticism). Morocco, Edition Erissāla, 1973.

of "*human beings*" and the spiritual upheaval the human civilization has experienced with the advent of Islam, passing through Islam's "*liberation*" of the human being from all forms of oppression. This liberation is stated through the first pillar of Islam, the "testimony of faith" (*shahāda*): "There is no god but God" [*lā illāha Illā Allāh*]. This formula expresses a negation of any supremacy other than the Creator of the Worlds. This testimony is the inexhaustible source of a liberating force that enables the believer to reject the hegemony of all other earthly deities, and to free his conscience from all carnal-passions like power, fame, and excessive materialism.

Through the testimony of faith, the human being, man or woman, frees himself and affirms his affiliation to human equality, which transcends social class, gender, and race. And through this testimony, he expresses his profound faith in divine justice. Thereby, the testimony of faith is inseparable from liberty, equality, and justice.

Thus, one cannot reconsider the issue of men and women without going back to the fundamental notions of ethics, repeatedly recommended to men and women believers, in the great majority of Qur'ānic verses. One must also consider the gradual comprehensive social reform and the social context of the time. Besides, the Qur'ān was revealed in twenty-three years, a rather short span of time radically to challenge prevailing sociocultural customs.

Nevertheless, the dynamics of the Revelation is characterized by unbroken instruction in the application of divine commandments, which explains the dramatic subsequent dissemination of the Qur'ānic message. Regarding women, the task was much more difficult, in view of the misogynist mindset of the period and the extent to which social behaviors regarding women had deteriorated, whether such deterioration resided in a tribal Arab milieu or within any other civilizations of the time.

Moreover, any interpretation of the scriptural sources, particularly those dealing with the relationship between men and women, should take into account several fundamental points: the general context of the spiritual message; the circumstances of the revealed verses in question; and the customs of the time, without forgetting the role played by the prophetic tradition which, in most cases, was one of the elements of articulating and translating the revelation on the basis of on-the-ground realities.

Using this approach, it becomes much easier, thenceforward, to consider the thematic of women within the setting of the spiritual message, to discern that the Qur'ān, ultimately and above all, is a word addressed to the human being, without distinctions of sex, race, or social status; a word that transcends gender; a universal call addressed to all humanity. Men and women are challenged in an egalitarian fashion, under different designations such as "O you believers" or "O you people," or "O you human beings." The complete spiritual equality is evidenced in the Qur'ān and is present throughout the Qur'ānic text, although it is often formulated as male, used as is the case in many languages, as gender neutral.[9] This neutrality has not prevented some Muslim women of the time, motivated by the liberating breath of the new spiritual message, from complaining directly to the Prophet about the tone of the Qur'ān being a little too "masculine." The Qur'ān's response did not take long to materialize, as seen in the revealed verses, in which the female gender is used in due and proper form as a response to these early feminine and feminists assertions:

> For submitting men and submitting women, believing men and believing women, devout men and devout women, truthful men and truthful women, patient men and patient women, humble men and humble women, charitable men and charitable women, men who fast and women who fast, men who guard their private parts and women who guard their private parts, men who remember God often and women who remember [God often], God has prepared forgiveness and a great reward.[10]

Thus, standing before their Creator, men and women are equal and are equally responsible for the protection and safeguard of the integrity of creation. This is one of the first fundamental principles that one finds in the Qur'ān, and which can, on it own, give a clear idea of the egalitarian vision of the spiritual message of Islam. The fact that the Qur'ān challenges men and women equally, at the time of revelation, in the year

[9]As we have seen in an earlier footnote (Chapter 3), "whether it is in reference to animate or inanimate objects, singular or plural, nouns in Arabic must indicate gender (feminine or masculine), with the masculine form being the default." As such, when male nouns, pronouns, or verbs are used to address a mixed group of people, it is understood to include all, males and females.

[10]The Qur'ān 33:35. For more details, see *Le Coran et les femmes, une lecture de liberation*.

610, is, in itself revolutionary! During this time, there was no place for women in any of the existing societies or religious traditions. And it was in this year of 610 that a spiritual revelation, carried forward by an unassuming man from Mecca, speaks about women in equal terms as men, as people who are morally and socially responsible. And there is more. The Qur'ān gives the example of women who marked the course of history. Thus, we find models of upright women as symbols of liberty, autonomy, and good governance, women who symbolize love, self-denial, and holiness.

We witness the example of Hagar, the second wife of the Prophet Abraham, a symbol of endurance and sacrifice, commemorated every year, for over fourteen centuries, in the rituals of the pilgrimage to Mecca.[11] Bilqīs is another woman the Qur'ān evokes, describing her as an intelligent and impartial ruler, endowed with great political skill and unparalleled wisdom, exposed in the manner in which she governed her empire. Other women are presented as symbols of resistance to tyranny, along the lines of the mother of Moses or of Asiya, the wife of Pharaoh, elevated to the rank of saint. And of course there is Mary (Mariam), the mother of Jesus, erected as a model of perfection and prophecy.[12]

These Qur'ānic narratives about women possess much more than historical significance. As such, they are of great importance not only for the time of the revelation, but also for our time, where women are often devalued for the simple reason of being women. The Qur'ānic stories about women have thus played a fundamental role in elevating the value of women in the eyes of a tribal society that had the custom of burying girls alive for fear of shame and dishonor![13]

Moreover, several verses in the Qur'ān motivate women to participate politically and socially, especially during the ceremonies of political allegiance (*Bay'a*). Thus, during oaths of allegiance, delegations of men and women concluded a pact with the Prophet of Islam as the representative of the Muslim community. During this period, the *Bay'a* was held to support the political representation of the leader. Here, we

---

[11] The ritual of *sa'y* consists of seven repeated courses, between the mountains of *Safa* and *Marwa*, during the pilgrimage to Mecca. Cf. *Le Coran et les femmes*, op. cit.

[12] Ibid.

[13] Isabelle Attané, *L'Asie manque de femmes*, which affirms that worldwide today, more than a hundred million women are missing, the vast majority in China and India, www.monde-diplomatique.fr/2006/07/ATTANE/13601.

see an imminent political act in which, fifteen centuries ago, women participated politically, in the name of Islam.[14] And women were given a political voice at a time of history when, a few years earlier, they were regarded as part and parcel of spoils of war, devalued, and disinherited for the simple reason of being women. Unfortunately, the important gains that women made during the Revelation have been usurped in the course of history, to the point that, even today, in a certain Islamic discourse, women are denied the right of political participation, justified by a completely erroneous interpretation of Islam!

The *hijra* (the migration of the Prophet and his followers from Mecca to Yathrib, later renamed Medina, by the Prophet) was another strong moment for the political engagement of women. The Qur'ān has encouraged them, just as much as men, to go into exile, in a difficult period of major conflicts between Muslims and the polytheists of Mecca.[15] Most of the women accepted such exile in the name of their faith and convictions, sacrificing families and children, in the service of their liberty and their political beliefs and choices. They have gone into exile, assuming through this act their proper place in the history of *hijra*, in the era of revelation, with all of its ups and downs, and bearing their share of suffering and sacrifice. History textbooks are full of names of women who have shaped the course of Islamic history at that time, examples that unfortunately were never perceived or appreciated at their real value.

Armed with all of this information from the time of revelation, Qur'ānic messages to the women but also to the men of the time should be reconsidered, in order to reformulate the question of the relationship between women and men, within the global vision of the Qur'ān. This Qur'ānic vision considers them both as custodians of an eternal promise, the promise to live on earth and to perpetuate the divine Creation in all of its splendor and beauty. Irrefutably, God created men and women as equal in liberty and in dignity. These are the fundamentals of equality that the sum of spiritual messages tried to convey to humanity, throughout centuries and centuries of history, but that, unfortunately, were always betrayed, paradoxically, in the names of these same religions.

---

[14] The Qur'ān 60:12.
[15] The Qur'ān 60:10.

The various religious interpretations have failed to highlight this equality; worse still, they have drained it of its spiritual essence, notwithstanding that women have always been, throughout the history of mankind, the main guardians of the faith.

To come back to the equality of men and women in the Qur'ān is to return, before all, to the key concepts of this equality, hence to the spiritual source of humanity, subtly described in the language of the Revelation as a universal declaration of human equality. This return to the source will take us back to the initial momentum of the Revelation, and accordingly we shall see how, in the time of Revelation, equality was, very simply, a reality, a concept that, today, is very hard to comprehend or believe.

PART II

Women and Men in the Qur'ān: The Key Concepts

CHAPTER 5

The Creation of Humanity

It is quite astonishing to see how the traditional version of the history of the creation of man remains the primary reference in any discussion about the origin of humanity. The predominant idea that Eve was created from Adam, with its full share of derogatory allegations about the first woman as a symbol of all sins, seems persistent in the collective imagination, no matter the religious tradition or the sociocultural context. In terms of their various interpretations of this idea, all religious traditions seem to merge in a way that defies time and space.

In the Old Testament, Eve is portrayed as being responsible for the fall of man[1]: "Sin began with a woman and because of her we must all die."[2] Concerning the Creation, two contradictory narrations are presented in the book of Genesis. In the first, men and women appear equal: "So God created man in His own image; in the image of God He created him; male and female He created them."[3] In the second, however, God would have said: "It is not good for the man to be alone. I will make a helper who is just right for him."[4] After Adam had fallen

---

[1] Arianne Buisset, *Les religions face aux femmes* (Edition Accarias, 2008), p. 22.

[2] The Book of Sirach 25:24. Catholics and some orthodox churches regard Sirach (Ecclesiasticus) as part of the sacred and canonical. The Book is preceded by a prologue that appears to have been written by the Greek translator of the original Hebrew text. Ecclesiasticus, The Catholic Encyclopedia, January 31, 2018.

[3] Genesis 1:27.

[4] Genesis 2:18.

© The Author(s) 2018
A. Lamrabet, *Women and Men in the Qur'ān,*
https://doi.org/10.1007/978-3-319-78741-1_5

in a deep sleep, the religious exegesis pronounces, Eve was created from one of his ribs.

Sadly, it is on the basis of this renowned assertion that all the religious interpretations coming from other traditions—Christianity and Islam—will rely to demonstrate the ontological inferiority of women. The "sacred" institution of misogyny begins with this second narrative of Genesis, whereas the first narration that speaks of the equal creation is to be forgotten, thus opening the way to a prolific religious literature that justifies the universal enslavement of women in the name of the sacred.

In Islam, despite the fact that the Qur'ān presents a completely different portrait, the classic exegeses (*tafāsīr*) are almost unanimous in reporting exactly the same interpretations used by prior religions. In fact, in the Qur'ān, the central verse that addresses this subject appears to present a completely different view of the creation of humanity: "O mankind! Reverence your Lord, Who created you from a single soul and from it created its mate, and from the two has spread abroad a multitude of men and women."[5]

Thus, one notes that the Qur'ānic text plainly attests to the spiritual equality, symbolized, as highlighted in the verse, by the creation story of women and men from the same essence, an expression that can be translated as the "original single soul." In a simple manner, this verse illustrates the different stages of the creation of humanity, from the original soul, from which its "alter ego" was formed, and from this couple, men and women who populated the earth were born. Nonetheless, most Muslim commentators of the classic epoch, echoing the spirit of other monotheist interpretations, end up reproducing the same categorical statements, identifying the original soul as Adam, the first man, and Eve, the partner derived from one of his ribs since, in the consciousness of the era, Adam is presumed to represent the ideal standard of humanity.

Many contemporary Muslim scholars and commentators have called into question this version, saying that "Adam" is a generic term that is often used in the Qur'ān in a broad sense to mean a "human being" or "Mankind." This is the explanation advanced by Muhammad 'Abduh, in his various writings, in which he contends that the name Adam refers to the individual or the human self.[6]

---

[5] The Qur'ān 4:1.

[6] *Tafsīr al-manār*, commentary on the first verse of *sūrah* 4. See also the excellent clarification given by the scholar Rashid al-Ghanushi in his book *Al-mar'a bayna al-Qur'ān wāqi' al-muslimīn*, The Maghreb Center for Research and Translation, 2000, London,

This newer reading thus affirms that humanity comes from a single origin and a single matter. The aim of the verse describing the creation would be to confirm the equality of the original human at every level. On the opposite side lies the classic interpretation, which interprets the term *nafs* (self) as a designation of the man or Adam and the term *zawj* (couple) to signify Eve or the first woman. For the reformists, however, the expression *nafs wāhida* designates the "original essence," whereas *zawj* signifies the "spouse," which reinforces and confirms the idea of an unconditional human equality without any consideration of gender or race.

Therefore, it seems that God created man and woman from a single substance, with these two human beings later constituting the sexual components of a single reality. This interpretation corresponds completely with the notion of the "duality" of the creation, which is repeatedly raised in the Qur'ān: "And of all things We have pairs, that haply ye may remember."[7] It is worthwhile to note that the previously cited verse (The Qur'ān 4:1) inaugurates one of the longest *sūrahs* in the Qur'ān, the *sūrah* of Women (*an-nisā'*), recognized as the fourth longest *sūrah* of the Sacred Text. The fact that this verse describing the creation is the opening of the *sūrah* whose title denotes women seems to show the importance of the symbolism of egalitarian creation in relation to the theme of women. The importance of this verse is also attested by traditional narrations reporting that the Prophet of Islam was in the habit of repeating this verse during most of his sermons.[8]

In his commentary, al-Rāzī explains that this verse constitutes, on its own, a general proclamation, destined to all humanity. He also signals that the immediately following verse speaks of orphans, especially young girls, but also of women, in addition to the oppressed on earth, which is not inadvertent, and must be understood as a major line of the Qur'ān, advocating the defense of the oppressed and disadvantaged minorities.[9] Al-Rāzī believes that this verse is to remind humans of a fundamental

p. 15. *Tafsīr al-manār* (12 volumes), in Arabic, can be downloaded at: https://archive.org/details/tfseer_manar.

[7] The Qur'ān 51:49.

[8] Reported by *Imām*, Ahmed and cited by Hanane Laham, *Min hady sūrat an-nisā'* (Dār al-Hudā, 1989).

[9] *Tafsīr Imām* Al-Rā-zī, *Mafātīh al-ghayb, at-tafsīr al-kabīr*.

notion, namely, their common origin. This, in his opinion, permits the avoidance of sinking into the negative properties of arrogance and pride and helps restore meaning to human modesty and humility.

This is also the conclusion arrived at by a prominent Muslim scholar, Muhammad Hussein Fadlallah, who likewise states that this verse is, above all, a call to all of humanity.[10] The opening of the verse, *yā ayyuhā an-nās*, "O mankind," designates all human beings, and it is there that we see one of the most important signs of the universality of the message of Islam.

In this oneness of the creation of the human race, there is a reflection of the human diversity that the Creator of the worlds intended. The creation account thus reminds us that human relationships are spiritual and that it is the same sentiment of spiritually that binds all beings, regardless of their origins, ethnicity, social classes, etc. A spiritual force connects men and women of this world and beyond, eternally together, notwithstanding their differences and despite their disagreements and disputes.

It is true that the traditionalist interpretation of this verse about the creation (Eve as subordinate to Adam) uses as reference a *hadīth* in which the Prophet describes the woman as having been "created from a bent rib that should at no point be forced for fear of breakage."[11]

Not surprisingly, many classic scholars call on some remark that the Prophet might have made, speaking of women in general, for the purpose of "forcing" a particular interpretation, especially regarding the verses that deal with the Creation, in order to draw the conclusion that women were created as subordinate to men. But studies of the prophetic traditions report that the cited *hadīth* was one among a group of recommendations in connection to the relations between men and women in seventh-century Arabia, in which the Prophet urged men to show kindness to women. The resemblance of these *hadīths* to the history of Adam and Eve reported in the biblical tradition will encourage these scholars to

---

[10] Muhammad Hussein Fadlallah (1935–2010) was a prominent Lebanese cleric and scholar. Born in Najaf, Iraq, where he spent two decades studying under leading Shia clerics, he returned to Lebanon in 1966. He was known for his liberal view of women, whom he believed equal to men in both capacities and responsibilities, and for having issued a *fatwa* (a nonbinding but authoritative legal opinion made by a religious authority) on the International Day for the Elimination of Violence against women that supports the right of women to defend themselves against all acts of violence.

[11] *Hadīth* reported by Abū Hurayra in the *Sahīh* of Bukhārī and the *Sahīh* of Muslim.

make the connection and from there deduce that Eve was created from one of Adam's ribs. As an aside, let us remember that at no point do the *hadīths* concerned suggest Adam. This interpretation is classically found in the majority of the work of the commentators of the Qur'ān, even though, as we have seen, there is no basis for it in the Qur'ān.

The *hadīth* invoking the rib was stated as part of a set of admonitions made by the Prophet to his companions during the Farewell pilgrimage where he encouraged them to treat women well. The use of the rib as an image—let us repeat once more that the Prophet was not talking about Adam's rib—was a metaphor, in the allegorical linguistic style that was very appreciated by the Arabs of the period, to recommend to men to show tact and kindness toward women.[12] As was his custom, the Prophet was trying to instill the rules of decency and consideration toward women and thereby appease the harsh mores of the time. It is therefore evident that all of the interpretations that use these *hadīths* to try to establish a secondary creation for women, in keeping with their devaluation, cannot be but wrong, as it flies in the face of the fundamental principles of the Qur'ān and the teachings of the Prophet.

Through the verse about the Creation and the concept of *nafs wāhida* (a single unified soul), the Qur'ān solemnly attests its total negation of all forms of segregation—be it racial, ethnic, sexual, or otherwise. This reminder, addressed to all of humanity, is worth reflecting upon at a moment when fratricidal wars and conflicts, not to mention environmental disasters, committed in the name of religion, dominance, and greed, flourish. While the Qur'ān persistently reminds humanity of its common origin, humans are killing each other to assert supremacy. The tragedy is that Muslims who are supposed to "bear witness" to the universality of their message walk past this sort of verse in total indifference, often retaining only some narrow and juvenile affirmations, such as the subordinate creation of Eve, as she is presumed to have been created from Adam, hence the "ordained" superiority of Man. Not only are these interpretations and commentaries wrong, they are also degrading to women and contrary to the Qur'ān's affirmation of the equality of God's human creations, in this world and the hereafter.[13]

---

[12] Rachid al-Ghannouchi, op. cit.

[13] It is important to remember that the designation Eve can be found nowhere in the Qur'ān. The name Adam, in turn, designates, according to the sense of the verse, the human being or the gender-neutral Man.

We must also remember that there is no mention in the Qur'ān of any responsibility by Eve for having been "chased out" of Paradise, and even a lesser notion of the original sin. All of the images of Eve as a temptress, a sinner, and the source of all evil, common to other monotheistic religious traditions, are absolutely absent from the Qur'ān. However, most of the exegeses (*tafāsīr*) and other commentaries on the Qur'ān reflect the same genre of discriminatory interpretations regarding the creation of the original human, which reveals the influence of the biblical literature on the medieval Islamic exegetical texts.[14]

In the Qur'ānic vision, the story of the Creation of Adam and Eve, as well as their fall from Paradise, reflects the joint responsibility of the two beings. The Qur'ān is very explicit when it comes to this shared responsibility by the two ancestors of humanity, Adam and Eve, in their disobedience of God, which also corresponds to their first awareness of liberty—the liberty to obey or disobey, the freedom to choose—the first consciousness of right and wrong and the first deliberate involvement of Mankind in earthly life.

Still, according to the Qur'ān, this first act of liberty and responsibility assumed by the first couple is, moreover, pardoned by the Creator after having them become aware of their human faculties, their differences and their similarities, their capacity to be free to reason. In other words, God teaches them to be equal and accountable men and women because they come from a same origin.

[14]See a detailed analysis on this theme in the work of Barbara Freyer Stowassar, *Women in the Qur'ān: Traditions, and interpretation* (Oxford University Press, 1994), p. 30.

CHAPTER 6

The Construction of Human Civilization

A key Qur'ānic concept that testifies to the intimate relationship of men and women with the Creator is that of *istikhlāf*, translated as the privilege offered by God to human beings, the privilege that symbolizes one of the most prestigious missions bequeathed to men and women: the construction of the human civilization on earth.

The notion of *istikhlāf* comes up under different forms multiple times in the Qur'ān. Commentators disagree regarding the various meanings of this term. However, judging by the context of the verses that call to mind this concept, one may distinguish at least three levels of meanings. In a general sense, the first level evokes the notion of "succession" (*khalīfa*), which gave birth to the term "caliphate," the *khalīfa* (caliph) being the "successor," or "he who occupies the position of another in a particular field."[1] The second, in its plural form *khalā'if*, designates the peoples, the tribes, or the generations that succeed one another. The third, still in the sense of succession, concerns the uniqueness of the management of the world, bestowed by God on humans:

> And when thy Lord said to the angels, "I am placing a vicegerent upon the earth," they said, "Wilt thou place therein one who will work corruption therein, and shed blood, while we hymn Thy praise and call Thee Holy?" He said, "Truly I know what you know not."[2]

[1] The Qur'ān 6:165; 10:14, 73; 2:30; 38:26.
[2] The Qur'ān 2:30.

© The Author(s) 2018
A. Lamrabet, *Women and Men in the Qur'ān*,
https://doi.org/10.1007/978-3-319-78741-1_6

This verse is regarded as pivotal in the design of the responsibility bequeathed by God on mankind.

Most commentators agree that this "representative" on earth, cited in the previous verse, refers to the human being (*banū Adam*) or the human race, in the first declaration by God that human beings should inhabit the earth.[3] It is a way of honoring human beings in giving them this symbolic function, consisting of "managing" what God has bequeathed. This "representation" is a privilege conferred only on human beings, not other creations. Indeed, human beings have a particular preeminence over the angels to the extent that, notwithstanding their spiritual superiority, the angels have not been considered worthy or perhaps up to the task of fulfilling this daunting assignment of managing the earth.

This explains the remark made by the angels to God: "Wilt thou place therein one who will work corruption therein, and shed blood, while we hymn Thy praise and call Thee Holy?" This remark has proven to be rather clairvoyant, given the disastrous management, by humans, of the natural resources of the earth and all the ravages committed throughout the history of mankind. The response of the Creator to the angels is categorical: "Truly I know what you know not." The creation of the human being, the will to accord him responsibility for the earth, with all that such responsibility entails in terms of tragedies, misery, but also creativity, all were to take place for a reason that is beyond our comprehension and which falls into these great mysteries that God alone knows: the significance of our presence on earth, the everlasting riddle that has been tormenting our poor human souls.

This *khilāfa*, or lieutenancy, granted by God to human beings is thus a without equal mark of regard, which renders mankind—endowed with reason and chosen by the Creator to accomplish the supreme function of populating the earth and organizing the modalities of his existence in the world—an invaluable and irreplaceable element within creation. Being

---

[3] Ismail ibn Kathir, *Tafsīr ibn Kathīr*, commentary on verse 30 of *sūrah* 2. Ismail ibn Kathīr (1300–1373) was a Syrian Sunni Muslim theologian and scholar best remembered for his fourteen-volume history of Islam, *Al-bidāyah wa al-nihāyah* ("The Beginning and the End"), and his well-known commentary on the Qur'ān, *Tafsīr al-Qur'ān al-Al'adhīm* ("The Interpretation of the Glorious Qur'ān"), in which he linked certain *hadiths* or sayings of the Prophet to verses of the Qur'ān in order to explain the meaning and intention of various verses and *sūrahs*.

the representatives of the divine will on earth is also and above all a huge responsibility—the preservation of the creation with all of its riches and natural resources. God offers human beings, men and women, the responsibility to utilize all of these earthly riches while avoiding wastefulness and abiding by the laws of nature in protection of its resources. As we see in a multitude of verses, the riches of His creation are a divine gift to humanity:

> Indeed, in the creation of the heavens and the earth; and the variation of the night and the day; and the ships that run upon the sea with what benefits mankind; and the water God sends down from the sky whereby He revives the earth after its death, scattering all manner of beast therein; and the shifting of the winds; and the clouds subdued between the sky and the earth are surely signs for a people who understand.[4]
>
> And He it is Who sends down water from the sky. Thereby We bring forth the shoot of every plant, and from it We bring forth vegetation from which We bring forth grain in closely packed rows; and from the date palm and from its sheaths, [We bring forth] clusters of dates hanging low, and gardens of grapes, olives, and pomegranates, like unto one another and yet not alike. Look upon their fruits, as they grow and ripen! Truly in that are signs for a people who believe.[5]

The Qur'ān encourages people to observe and reflect upon His signs—denoted in the Qur'ān as *āyāt*—so that they will always remember (*dhikr*) the primary responsibility for which they are created: to keep the earthly heritage bequeathed by the Creator of the worlds. Thus, the *khilāfa* is a deposit entrusted by God (*amāna*), a trust that must be understood and lived, day to day, by every man and every woman, each as an empowered and mindful captain, fully aware of the challenges of this great human adventure on earth.

To repeat, the *khilāfa*, in the Qur'ānic sense, is conditioned, first and foremost, by this responsibility, which must be carried out by every human being on earth. Human beings as *khalīfa* are not representatives of God on earth in the literal sense of the word; they are rather the custodians of the mission that the Creator has entrusted to them. They should therefore know how to revert to the original spiritual inspiration

[4] The Qur'ān 2:164.
[5] The Qur'ān 6:99.

and rediscover the original intent of the *khilāfa* in order to revive the sense of responsibility of men and women in this earthly life. This empowerment of human beings, men and women, also entails an ability that was "granted" to them: their liberty.[6] Responsibility and liberty go hand in hand, linked via a common ethic whereby one cannot go without the other.

Each time we discuss the equality of men and women and ponder its sociopolitical implications in the public space—equality in the liberty and responsibility to choose, to work, to manage, and to participate in the rapid growth of the world in which they live—we must remember this fundamental concept in the management of the world, as described in the Qur'ān. In the Qur'ānic text, the interpellation is clear. Life on earth cannot be adequately understood without taking into serious consideration the enormous responsibility that the Creator has laid upon us as human beings. It is true that the Qur'ānic teaching speaks of the eternal Divine Decree (*qadar*), but at the temporal level, the Qur'ān also affirms human responsibility.[7] This awareness is essential for the rejuvenation of the egalitarian spirit of the spiritual message that empowers men and women equally and without differentiation, with each one of us, man and woman, being a custodian of this divine gift, and guardian of the treasures of the earth. So, throughout his or her life on earth, every human being, man and woman, represents the divine will. And it is the degree of our consciousness regarding the heavy divine deposit that testifies to our spiritual commitment to preserve life on earth. A human mindfulness of the responsibility or the *khilāfa* is reflected in the extent of exemplary concern for the effectiveness and excellence (*ihsān*) of human actions. In fact, several Qur'ānic verses evoke the concept of *khilāfa* in close equation with "good action" (*al-'amal as-sālih*), faith (*al-īmān*), but also generosity and altruism (*al-infāq*).[8]

Furthermore, this responsibility for the earth, bestowed on the human being, is also important because it is what keeps us in check, in regard to

[6] Souleymane Bachir Diagne speaks of this liberty, which manifests itself at the inception of the human being: "the Qur'ānic story of the appearance of human beings seems to recognize that he is the custodian of a treasure that only he can manifest: freedom," in *Comment philosopher en islam?* (Edition de Panama, 2008).

[7] More than 300 verses of the Qur'ān speak about mankind's responsibility regarding his own actions (9:120; 49:19; 47:33).

[8] The Qur'ān 24:55; 57:7.

the quality of the human management of our world, at a time when, on multiple levels, the planet suffers from serious imbalances, including economic crises and climatic changes, perhaps early warning signs of what is to come. The upshot of this globally advertised crisis is evident—a material and moral bankruptcy—in short, our undeniable shared responsibility for the chaos in which we live. We have but to look around us to be able to perceive the extent of the damage perpetrated in the name of human civilization and to realize that we have failed in carrying out our primary responsibility as humans—the sound preservation of what God has left in our hands as a deposit, a treasure to protect, an *amāna*.

In this sense, it is urgent that we reinvigorate the memory of *khilāfa*, engraved in the depths of our human consciousness, to allow it to manifest itself through our daily actions. Reclaiming this responsibility means revitalizing the remembrance of spiritual dignity and the responsible liberty that God has granted us, as men and women, to accomplish, in an exemplary fashion, a mission intrinsic to our humanity.

CHAPTER 7

Moral Integrity as an Evaluation Criteria

O mankind! Truly We created you from a male and a female, and We made you peoples and tribes that you may come to know one another. Surely the most noble of you before God are the most reverent of you. Truly God is Knowing, Aware. (The Qur'ān 49:13)

The previous Qur'ānic verse carries major importance because it assesses the intrinsic value of human beings, men or women. It should be noted that, from the start, the verse opens with an explicit reference to humans, of the common origin, that of a man and a woman from whom multitudes of tribes and nations were established. The extreme diversity of these peoples could make one forget the common origin and the unity of creation.

God has created peoples and nations, with all of their specificities, their differences, their cultures, and their modes of living. From this unity, God created diversity as a challenge to humans: live your diversity and accept others in their differences. Does this not pose a challenge to our modern egocentrism? Qur'ānic encouragement of mutual understanding among peoples invites mutual enrichment through openness toward the Other, regardless of their difference, ethnicity, or culture of origin. The mutual understanding that the Qur'ān speaks of is that of the enrichment of the human experience, constantly, eternally, via contributions made by the Other, with his or her specific traits, with each party offering the best it has: "Surely the most noble of you before God are the most reverent of you." God does not differentiate among the human beings whom he created different. Be it a man or a woman, no one can

© The Author(s) 2018
A. Lamrabet, *Women and Men in the Qur'ān*,
https://doi.org/10.1007/978-3-319-78741-1_7

claim a special consideration in the eyes of the Lord. There are no chosen peoples or privileged nations.

The equality of all human beings in the eyes of the Creator is absolute, transcending all particularities, race, ethnicity, skin color, or sex. The sole merit in the eyes of God is that which the Qur'ān defines in this verse as *taqwā*. But what does *taqwā* really signify? From an etymological viewpoint, the term *taqwā* entails a sense of restraint and of conservation. The Prophet defined *taqwā* as an inner-core quality. In a well-known *hadīth* regarding *taqwā*, the Prophet affirms "the *taqwā* is here, the *taqwā* is here, the *taqwā* is here," pointing to his heart with his hand and repeating the phrase three times.[1]

'Umar Ibn al-Khattāb, the second *rashidūn* (rightly guided) Caliph and one of the Prophet's earliest companions, once asked a companion, Ubayy Ibn Ka'b, to explain to him the sense of *taqwā*. "Let's assume that one day," Ubayy said, "you find yourself on a road that is covered with thorns—what would you do?" 'Umar responded: "I would roll up my sleeves and I would endeavor to avoid these thorns," at which point Ubayy said: "Well, the *taqwā* is that!"[2]

The term *taqwā* is frequently described as "piety." Traditionally, *taqwā* has been mostly confined within the strict domain of worship and individual morality. It is also often identified as religious demeanor, characteristic of those who belong to a mystical movement that advocates withdrawal from the world. For them, *taqwā* is the fear of God, or as some have called it, "reverent awe" of God.

It is true that *taqwā* can be equated to piety, to fear, or to fear of the Creator, as it is a common feeling that animates the hearts of practitioners; all religions have insisted on the link between the practice of a cult and the fear of divine punishment. All of those sentiments are utterly human and spontaneous, inherent to human nature (*fitra*), which is nothing other than this imprint of the presence of God buried in the depths of our souls. But *taqwā* cannot be reduced to piety and fear alone. In fact, it has two critical dimensions, one interior in the hearts of believers, as has been described by the Prophet, the other exterior, which

---

[1] A *hadīth* transmitted by the Prophet's companion 'Abd ar-Rahmān Ibn Sakhr (known as Abu Hurairah) and cited by Abū Tahar As-Salafy, *Al-mashīkha al-baghdadiyya*, vol. 23.

[2] *Tafsīr Ibn Kathīr*, commentary on verses 2 and 3 of *sūrah* 2: "This is the book in which there is no doubt, a guidance for the reverent, who believe in the Unseen and perform the prayer and spend from that We have provided them."

consists precisely of the externalization of this internal quality through acts and demeanor that reflect this virtue of the heart. In other words, according to the clarification given by Ubbay, it is, above all, the personal effort endeavored by every man and every woman to confront life's challenges and trials.

In the first place, *taqwā* should be understood and lived as a spiritual value of love and of respect of God, which should be put into practice in one's daily life. It is also the unceasing openness of the spirit that aspires toward the Creator. It is becoming closer to God through acts of virtue. It is the awareness of always being with God, everywhere, through one's heart and acts.

The Qur'ān thus insists on the equality of all human beings, the only differentiating factor among them being the degree of their *taqwā*, understood in its pluralist and open way and not as some have understood it in a restrictive sense of passive devotion, fatalist and futile. *Taqwā* does in fact involve being devoted to the Creator and to submit to His commands, but through devotion that knows how to remain alive, active, and creative, and this can be realized only in the understanding and knowledge of both faith and reason. In this sense, *taqwā* corresponds to a profound need of liberty—adhering to faith to free the mind from material futilities and negative passion, thus enabling it to reach infinite freedom. One may say that a pious man feels profoundly free. As Rousseau stated: "Make me free by protecting me against those of my passions which do violence to me. Prevent me from being their slave; force me to be my own master and to obey not my senses but my reason."[3]

In their endeavor to reach *taqwā*, men and women must strive to merit such state of being. At the end, there is nothing but this spirituality that becomes, through effort and merit, a liberating force, a force that releases the faithful, men and women, from the chains of excessive materialism and lifts them to the very top of the skies of freedom. The best of all men and all women in front of God are those who know how to free themselves from their passions, their egos, and who will make the most effort to do, in this life, as many good deeds as possible for others, all others, regardless of origin, color, or race. This is the illustration of one of the finest forms of equality that is done in liberty, with the commitment of the heart and the dedication to action.

---

[3] Jean-Jacques Rousseau, *The sentiment of existence* (Cambridge University Press, 2006).

CHAPTER 8

The Egalitarian Call of the Qur'ān

It is recognized that the major part of the Qur'ān calls on both men and women without distinction via different formulations such as *an-nās* (the people), *banī Adam* (the children of Adam), *qawm* (community), or *umma* (nation). Qur'ānic injunctions, expressed in the masculine voice, such as *yā ayyuha al-mu'minūn* ("O you believers"), systematically encompass women in the quasi-unanimous opinion of the *'ulamā* (Muslim scholars), who agree that the divine word, apart from some formulas that are specifically addressed to one or the other of the sexes, concerns both men and women without any differentiation.[1]

Except for verses that specifically address men, the masculine tense in the Qur'ān is gender neutral and suggests human universality. For example, when a term such as *rijāl*, which normally denotes men, is used in the Qur'ān, it designates an elite group of men and women, such as the term "mankind" in English.

A *hadīth* reported in the works of classic Muslim scholars explicitly reveals how, early on in the Qur'ānic revelation, women enthusiastically assimilated the egalitarian principle of the new spiritual message. In this regard, it is narrated that Umm Salama, the wife of the Prophet, also known as "the mother of believers" (*umm al-mu'minīn*), was one day

---

[1] Regarding the question of equality in the Qur'ān, it is affirmed by a large number of Muslim scholars, including Ibn Rushd (Averroes), Ibn al-Qāyyim, and Ibn 'Arabī. See, for comparison, Abū Shuqqa, *Taḥrīr al-mar'ā fi 'asr ar-risāla*, 7th ed. (Dār al-Qalam, 2011), p. 70.

A. Lamrabet, *Women and Men in the Qur'ān*,
https://doi.org/10.1007/978-3-319-78741-1_8

washing herself with the aid of a servant girl when she heard a call that summoned believers to an urgent meeting in the Medina mosque, under the patronage of the Prophet. She immediately stood up and hastened to prepare herself to go join this general convocation, under the astonished gaze of her servant, who pointed out that the call was addressed to the people (*an-nās*), which in principle concerned only men. Umm Salama quickly retorted, "I am one of the people" (*anā min an-nās*).[2] Like all other women at the dawn of Islam, she fully realized that the spiritual message concerned her as much as it concerned men. As a Muslim woman of the first hour, engaged in the front ranks of Muslims who fought body and soul for Islam, she considered the attendance of such a public meeting, led by the Prophet, an opportunity to exercise her legitimate right of social participation in the company of other male and female believers.

In parallel with most verses that call on men and women without distinction, there are a few verses, exactly six in number, that are addressed to both men and women but in a formulation that specifies the masculine and feminine genders, as we see in the following verse, highlighted earlier in the book:

> For submitting men and submitting women, believing men and believing women, devout men and devout women, truthful men and truthful women, patient men and patient women, humble men and humble women, charitable men and charitable women, men who fast and women who fast, men who guard their private parts and women who guard their private parts, men who remember God often and women who remember [God often], God has prepared forgiveness and a great reward.[3]

What we witness here is a clear demonstration of the symmetrical equality, repeated in several other verses, of men and women believers in terms of their participation (ritual and action) and shared responsibility in this life and the hereafter. By specifically calling each man and each woman, the Qur'ān asserts the total equality of believers, the only distinction among them being the strength of one's conviction, not the sex of the

---

[2] A *hadīth* reported in *Sahīh Muslim* by Ahmad Ibn Hanbal, who founded the Hanbali school, one of the four main Sunni schools of jurisprudence. The other three schools are Hanafi, Māliki, and Shafi'i.

[3] The Qur'ān 33:35.

believer. Moreover, by examining the verse in terms of the particular circumstances of the revelation, we can also better understand not only the objectives of the verse but also the underlying spirit of the particular style of this verse.

In most classic exegetical compilations (*tafāsīr*), there are several versions concerning the circumstances of the revelation of this verse; they all converge, however, in terms of its purpose—a response to a "feminine complaint." Indeed, all versions agree that the verse was an unwavering response to an inquiry and request made by a large number of women who had been rather "saddened" by the Qur'ānic discourse that, at least initially, seemed to ignore them and address only men. One of the most famous versions of the narrations is that of the aforementioned Umm Salama, the wife of the Prophet, who one day asked him: "Why are we, women, not addressed in the Qur'ān as are the men?" That very day, at the hour of the noon prayer, they heard the Prophet announcing, from his pulpit, the descent of the verse cited previously (The Qur'ān 33:35).

According to a slightly different version, Umm Salama said: "Why are men cited all the time, and we women are not?"[4] Yet another version reports that it was one of the wives of the Prophet, without specifying which one, who said: "Why does God mention men believers, but not women believers?" Always coming from the same position and nature of the objection, another version is attributed to other women of the Muslim community, such as Umm 'Amara al-Ansāriyya, who was reported as having said: "We see that all is in favor of men, and that women are hardly mentioned by the word of God!"[5]

According to Ibn 'Ashūr, the petitioner was none other than Asmā' bint Umays, who, having just returned from Abyssinia (present-day Ethiopia) in the company of a number of other Muslim women, all of whom had been living there in exile, complained to the Prophet on behalf of the entire group of women: "We women are very saddened to see that we are not cited in the Qur'ān, as are the men!"[6] All of these grievances, expressed by different women or groups of women and confirmed by several sources, testify to the important presence of women during this period and to their strong commitment to the ongoing

---

[4] *Tafsīr at-Tabarī, hadīth* of Mujāhid.

[5] *Tafsīr Ibn Kathīr, hadīth* reported by an-Nasā'ī.

[6] Ibn 'Ashūr, *Tafsīr at-tahrīr wa at-tanwīr.*

sociopolitical process under the leadership of Islam, which for them was an important spiritual force of mobilization.

The conduct of these women of the first community confirms the historical information of the era that chronicles the visible presence of women in all of the major events that marked this period. The feminine demand was nothing short of a legitimate questioning by these women, wanting to understand, with precision, their correct place in the Qur'ānic discourse, thereby confirming their role as equal partners alongside men. This feminine demand of this first hour also illustrates the birth of a new female consciousness, informed and fully aware of its rights and responsibilities—rights and responsibilities granted to them directly and officially by the liberating message of Islam.

These first Muslim women actively participated in the erection of the first city of Islam under the protection and with the unconditional encouragement and support of the Prophet, who not only was one of the greatest defenders of the female cause but also of all the oppressed on earth. Needless to say, women were among the most oppressed minorities during this period. These women, therefore, sacrificed themselves, sometimes at the risk of their own lives, for the edification of the new spiritual message. In exile, they gave the best of themselves—dedication, separation from their loved ones, insecurity, poverty, sufferance, all of which they accepted with joyous and hopeful hearts, knowing they were now free, autonomous, and independent. Islam had given these women a new social status as human beings, dignified, free, and on equal footing as men.

This is exactly why these women protested and complained to the Prophet; they were exercising their newly acquired rights and wanted to be directly addressed in the Qur'ān in the same fashion as men; and even though, deep down, they knew full well that the Divine had not ignored them and that which had been newly revealed involved them as much as it did men, they wanted to be reassured. In this context, the dawn of Islam, what could have been more natural for these women, triumphant in terms of their newly acquired rights, than to assert their presence by actively seeking clear answers to their aspirations? They rightly felt a need for such confirmation, an ultimate testimony by the Creator of all, in his Eternal Book, reaffirming their equal status as women via their direct mention in the Qur'ān rather than being content to be submerged in the general concept of "believers."

And this is exactly what the Qur'ān confirmed by punctuating the verse with the specification of men and women believers—an undeniable recognition by the Creator of the equal engagement of men and women, a clear response to a challenge that resulted from a feminine demarche that questioned the sacred text in a most direct and natural way. And the Qur'ān responded to the demand through a verse that indisputably defined the egalitarian foundation of the relationship between men and women. In this regard, let us once again pause to remember that it is seventh-century Arabia we are talking about, with its very deep patriarchal roots. What better argument than what we have already seen to convince those in doubt that, in its egalitarian viewpoint regarding men and women, the Qur'ān was indeed a pioneer.

While the strong egalitarian outlook of this Qur'ānic verse is evident, it has not been awarded the attention it deserves within the compendium of Islamic writing (*tafāsīr*). This is particularly appalling given that it would be impossible to find any discussion of equality in Islam as eloquently articulated in verse 33:35. Through this verse that addresses men and women, the Qur'ān highlights the breadth of their conviction (*īmān*), the serenity of their hearts (*khushū'*), their sincerity (*sidq*), and their capacity to be patient (*sabr*), a mature patience that can withstand obstacles because of its confidence in God, a patience that has been erected within the persistence of its relentless struggle against oppression, not a forced patience generated by the inevitability of submission to injustice. We also see an emphasis on humility and a demonstration of bounty and generosity, all generated by their unwavering faith. These are men and women who knew how to give themselves up in the service of others (*ihsān*) as an act of profound piety and to fast (*sawm*) as a true purification of the soul rather than a mundane deprivation of the body. The verse also evokes those men and women who are virtuous and who exercise restraint and decency, inside and outside, manifested in modesty (*hayā'*) of soul and self. The Prophet, known to have been bashful, describes bashfulness as "one of the branches of faith."[7] And God speaks of "men who remember God often and women who remember [God often]" (*adh-dhākirīn wa adh-dhākirāt*), and whose reminiscence and evocation of the Creator and His creation is part and parcel of their daily worship—those (men and women) who never forget the sense of

---

[7] "Faith consists of seventy-seven branches and bashfulness is one of these branches," as reported in *Sahīh al-Bukhāri* and *Sahīh Muslim*.

their presence on earth and who reflect on the meaning of their transient passage through this world, the meaning of life, of death, and who never forget their destiny in the hereafter.

In this sense, the Prophet highlights the importance of this virtue—the remembrance of God. The Prophet was asked one day: "Who are the human beings considered best in the eyes of God?" Using gender-specific language, the Prophet responded: "Those [men and women] who invoke the name of the Creator frequently" (*adh-dhākirīna wa adh-dhākirāt*).[8] It is evident that the invocation of the name of God should not be superficial, done orally without the engagement of the heart, and certainly not without a profound consciousness of His presence in our daily lives, in our conduct toward others, in our way of being. Remembering God is in the perfection of our acts, our words; it is the constant striving for honesty and moral integrity in respect and deference toward Him who sees everything and who is nearer to us than our own "jugular vein" and who knows our deepest intimacies[9]; to remember God is to be with Him, and to be with Him is to be with all others.

Thus, through this verse, the Qur'ān stipulates that men and women are judged by the Creator, not by their masculine or feminine gender but by their actions, their sincerity, their honesty, their piety, their respective contributions to the society in which they live, coexist, and help each other for the Common Good.

In addition to this verse, there are five others where one finds the same egalitarian imperative between men and women:

> Whosoever works righteousness, whether male or female, and is a believer, We shall give them new life, a good life, and We shall surely render unto them their reward in accordance with the best of that which they used to do.[10]
>
> And whosoever performs righteous deeds, whether male or female, and is a believer, such shall enter the Garden, and they shall not be wronged so much as the speck on a date-stone.[11]

---

[8] *Hadīth* reported by Ahmad.

[9] The Qur'ān 50:16: "We did indeed create man and We know what his soul whispers to him; and We are nearer to him than his jugular vein."

[10] The Qur'ān 16:97.

[11] The Qur'ān 4:124.

So their Lord answered them, I shall not let the work of any worker among you, male or female, be in vain; each of you is like the other. So those who emigrated, and were expelled from their homes, and were hurt in My way, and fought and were slain—I shall absolve them of their evil deeds and shall make them enter Gardens with rivers running below, a reward from God. And God, with Him is the most beautiful reward.[12]

Whosoever commits an evil deed will not be requited, save with the like thereof; but whosoever, whether male or female, performs a righteous deed and is a believer shall enter the Garden wherein they will be provided for without reckoning.[13]

Truly men who give in charity and women who give in charity, and lend unto God a goodly loan, it will be multiplied for them, and theirs shall be a generous reward.[14]

These five verses demonstrate the high degree of the Qur'ān's insistence on an egalitarian vision by punctuating, as we have seen earlier, each of these verses with indicators that make it abundantly clear that the call is addressed, at once, to both men and women. In His infinite splendor, God promises men and women, in an identical manner, never to cause them to lose the value of their actions and toil on earth; they will be compensated accordingly and will enjoy the favors of their Creator.

In one of these verses, by reiterating the egalitarian principles of Divine judgment, the Qur'ān reminds us that this principle of equality derives from the original egalitarian nature of the creation of men and women, as we have seen in verse 195 of *surah* 3, "You proceed one from another," which is layered with the notion of equality being linked to all aspects of their lives, spiritual and temporal. This point has been raised by certain classic exegeses, affirming that the expression "of any worker, male or female" together with "You proceed one from another" testify to the insistence of the Creator concerning this notion of equality, which is, furthermore, reinforced by the image of men and women proceeding from one another.[15]

This Qur'ānic metaphor attests to the intensity of this union that connects one to another, in short, women to men, ensued one from another, which confirms the principle of the common origin of all humans. The Qur'ānic

[12] The Qur'ān 3:195.

[13] The Qur'ān 40:40.

[14] The Qur'ān 57:18.

[15] Al-Baydāwī, *Anwār at-tanzīl wa asrār at-ta'wīl*, commentary on verse 195 of *surah* 3.

message is a reminder that there could be no differentiation in the treatment or in judgment, in this world or the hereafter, among beings originating from the same creation and the same origin.

Many classic commentators affirm that this verse is the equivalent of another, where the equality of the sexes is also strongly affirmed: "But the believing men and believing women are protectors of one another, enjoining right and forbidding wrong, performing the prayers, giving the alms, and obeying God and His messenger. They are those upon whom God will have mercy. Truly God is Mighty, Wise."[16] Continuing with verse 195 of *sūrah* 3, the exegetic tradition informs us that it was Umm Salama who was the origin of the revelation.[17] She is narrated to having said to the Prophet, "Men are mentioned in the Qur'ān numerous times for their participation in the immigration (*hijra*) while we the women have not been addressed in the sacred text regarding the *hijra*!"

To comprehend the pertinence of her remark, it will suffice to remember the historic role that she herself played in the edification of the first Muslim community, especially during some of the most difficult periods, such as the *hijra* (migration; exile). In fact, the first male and female believers had no choice but to seek exile from Mecca in order to avoid the reprisals that the polytheists of Quraysh[18] subjected them to because of their religious convictions. The request of Umm Salama was doubly comprehensible: In fact, it is she who was nicknamed "the woman of the two exiles" by the Islamic tradition because she had been forced to migrate twice, once to Abyssinia and then to Medina. History even reports that she was the first woman to migrate to Abyssinia.

After settling in Medina, Umm Salama, the spouse of the Prophet and "the Mother of believers," is expressing her sadness, perhaps even her disappointment to see that the Qur'ān had glossed over, even ignored her sacrifice as well as the sacrifices of the women with her, in this forced exile. They had almost lost their lives and were deprived of their children in order to protect their faith and commitment to Islam. So it was within

---

[16] The Qur'ān 9:71.

[17] Ibn Kathīr's commentary.

[18] The Quraysh were the dominant mercantile tribe of Mecca and controlled its *Ka'ba*, which was a significant source of wealth because of the yearly pilgrimage that Arab tribes made to Mecca. The tribe was divided into ten main clans, including Hāshim, the Prophet's own clan. Until they converted to Islam in 630, the Quraysh were among the most zealous enemies of Muhammad and his new revelation.

this context that the verse was revealed as a clear response to the request of Umm Salama and, through her, to all the women and men:

> So their Lord answered them, I shall not let the work of any worker among you, male or female, be in vain; each of you is like the other. So those who emigrated, and were expelled from their homes, and were hurt in My way, and fought and were slain—I shall absolve them of their evil deeds and shall make them enter Gardens with rivers running below, a reward from God. And God, with Him is the most beautiful reward.

In this way, the verse also responds to the men and women who were still reluctant to recognize the egalitarian vision of the last message of God. Even though, from the beginning, the Revelation has always addressed all humans, be they men or women, this request of Umm Salama was an opportunity to renew the egalitarian principle of Islam that women and men are fundamentally equal in their spiritual and temporal commitment. "I shall not let the work of any worker among you, male or female, be in vain; each of you is like the others" is a divine recognition and a solemn promise coming from the Creator to humanity in its entirety. It is an eternal promise that defies time, space, and history, a promise that should be incorporated into all of our Islamic educational manuals as a lifetime ethic to be taught to our children and future generations so that this culture of equality is understood, assimilated, considered, experienced, and lived as an essential foundation of the message of Islam.

CHAPTER 9

The Qur'ānic Ethic of the Marital Union

QUR'ĀNIC DIRECTIONS CONCERNING MARRIAGE

Throughout the Qur'ān, one finds numerous directives concerning the marital union in Islam. The values and principles of this union are laid down in several *sūrahs*, sometimes in isolation, other times regrouped in the form of strong recommendations. This is the case of the verses that follow which, while they do not summarize the entire body of the Qur'ānic ethic concerning marriage, reflect a set of overarching concepts that are essential for an adequate understanding of the Qur'ānic philosophy regarding marital union.

> O you who believe! It is not lawful for you to inherit women through coercion, nor to prevent them from marrying [again] that you may take away some of what you have given them, unless they commit a flagrant indecency. And consort with them in a kind and honorable way; for if you dislike them, it may be that you dislike a thing in which God has placed much good. If you desire to take one wife in place of another, even if you have given to one of them a great sum, take back nothing from it. Would you take it by way of calumny and manifest sin? And how can you take it back, when you have lain with one another, and they have made with you a solemn covenant?[1]

[1] The Qur'ān 4:19–21.

© The Author(s) 2018
A. Lamrabet, *Women and Men in the Qur'ān*,
https://doi.org/10.1007/978-3-319-78741-1_9

It is important to note here that these verses, as some others in the Qur'ān, are addressed specifically to men, and in a strong reprimanding tone. As we have already noted, while the Qur'ān is fundamentally a universal message, it often specifically challenges Arab men of Hijāz, in the Arabian Peninsula, for their notorious discourteous and disrespectful behavior toward women.

The first verse starts by forbidding a pre-Islamic tribal custom that treated women as objects, an integral part of inheritance. In fact, during this period, it was customary for families to include widows in the inheritance that is acquired by the in-laws. The woman whose husband had died found herself appropriated by one of the male members of her in-laws—father, brother, or even a distant cousin of the deceased—who, as of that moment, would consider her his property, his right, his inherited "thing." These women were under the guardianship of their in-laws, unable to circulate freely or, God forbid, begin a new life elsewhere.[2]

In his commentary, Ibn Kathīr reports that the verse was revealed specifically for a woman named Kubaysha bint Ma'n Asim, of the tribe of Aus. The woman had come to complain to the Prophet that, at the death of her husband, she was forced to stay under the guardianship of her stepson who did not permit her either to inherit from her dead husband or to re-marry. Other women of Medina, having heard of this complaint, came to the Prophet in droves to complain about the same sort of thing.[3] This was how the Revelation formally forbidding this discriminatory custom that violated the individual liberty and dignity of women came about.

In his *tafsīr*, another commentator, Zamakhsharī, commented on the verse by way of a bitter statement about the social conditions of women of the period, women who, at the death of their husbands, suffered the worse types of discrimination, including the appropriation of their money and any other material possessions they might have had. Some were even confined until their death.[4]

Pursuant to this verse, the Qur'ān equally condemns husbands from among the believers who, using threats and intimidations, oblige their

[2] More or less, classical exegeses report the same sort of facts. See, especially, *Tafsīr Ibn Kathīr.*

[3] Abū al-Hassan an-Nīsābū, *Asbāb an-nuzūl* (Dār al-Jayl, 2002).

[4] Al-Zamakhsharī, *Tafsīr al-Kashshāf.* Known as *Al-Kashshāf* (the Revealer), the book is a seminal *tafsīr* written in the twelfth century.

wives to relinquish all of their possessions, including their *mahr*, and any other gifts they might have received. Thus, these women were forced to abandon everything for the benefit of those who had grown tired of them and then stripped them of all their property.[5]

The Qur'ānic expression utilized here is *wa lā ta'dulūhunna*, which is translated as "do not subject them to restraints." This prohibition encompasses all constraints, pressures, and violence, whether physical or verbal, against these women as a means of forcing them to surrender the totality of their property, including the *mahr* received from the husband at the moment of the marriage contract. The only exception that allows the return of the *mahr* to the husband is when the wife is found guilty of adultery (*fāhisha mubīna*). In such a case, the husband can oblige his wife to give him back his due, since it is he who has suffered injury.[6] Apart from this justification, a husband has no right to touch any of the material possessions of his wife, whether it is the *mahr*, personal property, or any other legacy that is an integral part of her private property.

In his commentary, Ibn Kathīr interprets this verse as follows: "Do not constrain your wives and do not make it impossible for them to live with you for the sole purpose of depriving them of what you have given them, or make them concede to you by submitting them to the worst oppressions and offenses, and assaulting their inalienable rights, which you, as a husband, must protect."[7] Ibn Kathīr has also reported that during this period, some men no longer desire to continue living with their wives mistreated them and made them suffer much brutalities and prejudices. The objective of this abuse was to force the wives to relinquish their *mahr* in exchange for their liberty. In short, men were thus able to extort the assets of their wives and then push them out of the matrimonial residence—a total physical and material dispossession. And Zamakhsharī has acknowledged the same—that women suffered enormous discrimination, and submitted to all forms of injustice, due to this type of conduct and the abuse of power practiced by some men.[8]

As we have seen, this Qur'ānic verse cannot be clearer in terms of its formal prohibition of the infliction of any type of injustice on women.

[5] *Tafsīr Ibn Kathīr*, verse 4:19.

[6] *Tafsīr* Muhammad Hussein Fadlallah.

[7] Ibid.

[8] Al-Zamakhsharī, *Tafsīr al-Kashshāf* of verse 4:19.

And it is indeed abuse in different shapes and forms that the Qur'ānic verse is prohibiting, the type of abuse that has been the subject of discussion by major international conventions. For example, the Council of Europe defines intra-familial abuse as "any act or omission that undermines the life, the physical or psychological integrity, or the liberty of a family member, or that seriously harms the development of his or her personality or hinders his or her financial security, committed by another member of the same family."[9]

Unfortunately, this type of abuse is not restricted to a particular period. In fact, it has persisted through time and is considered among the most serious tragedies that many contemporary societies, including Muslim societies, endure. How many women in our times continue to suffer this type of abuse that forces them to abandon all—their own earned wealth, savings, children, homes, shared property—in exchange for liberty. And how many Muslim men are subjecting their wives to extreme physical and psychological violence to be able to extract their wealth and then throw them out into the street?

These verses are therefore addressed to all men as a reminder of their obligations vis-à-vis their partners but also and above all as an unconditional directive to respect the property of their spouses and to treat it as sacrosanct. Here, the Qur'ān insists that, even in cases of dispute, unless the wife approves, but not under duress, a husband does not have the right to touch his wife's personal assets. The reference to the *mahr* in this verse is but a specific measure to emphasize the importance that the Qur'ān accords to the personal property of the wife, and thus, to her material independence. In fact, the Qur'ān here expresses the prohibition of depriving wives of their rights, in general, especially their economic rights, represented at that time by the *mahr* that the bride receives as a present from her husband.

Here, it is indispensable to clarify the concept of *mahr*, translated loosely as dowry, which is rather vague and misleading to most people, both Muslims and non-Muslims. *Mahr* is "the amount of money paid by the groom to the bride, at the time of marriage … to show that he [the groom] has a serious desire to marry her and is not … entering into

---

[9] Site of the Ministry, *du travail, de la solidarité et de la fonction publique*, http://travail-soldarité.gouv.fr.

the marriage contract without any sense of responsibility. ... It isn't the bride's price or her value but a gift to her."[10]

Thus, the term *mahr* in Islam does not correspond to either dowry, as it is understood in the West, or a bride's price. One of the most persistent prejudices toward Islam is the belief that a Muslim man "buys" his spouse from her father, a completely false assertion. When the term "dowry" is used in the Islamic context, it should be strictly understood as a description of the negotiations between the families of the future bride and groom, particularly the exchange of cash or kind by the bride and groom and/or their families.

Throughout the world, dowry is conceived differently on the basis of the cultures and social norms of different peoples. For some, it is the husband who must present a dowry to the family of the future bride; for others, it is the family of the bride that is obliged to offer the dowry to the future husband. Dowry is also mentioned in the early texts of the Bible. For example: "If a man seduces a virgin who is not betrothed and lies with her, he shall give the bride-price for her and make her his wife. If her father utterly refuses to give her to him, he shall pay money equal to the bride-price for virgins."[11] And a contemporary Rabi has written:

> Originally, in Judaism, when a young man wanted to marry, he was required to buy his wife from her father (today, this custom is even practiced by the Muslims). *This payment, was in money or livestock or work, and was called the* "MOHAR." Later, the MOHAR was paid to the bride and not the father. Later on, the MOHAR became a written commitment named "KÉTOUBA" by which the husband promised his wife a sum of money in case of divorce or death.[12]

In India, in contrast, it is the bride's family that must pay a dowry to the groom, a custom that provokes tragedies for the families not positioned to be able to honor this obligation. In fact, if the dowry were considered inadequate, the wife could become the victim of deadly violence. Despite the official interdiction of such custom in 1961, it remains the norm.

[10] http://islamic-dictionary.tumblr.com/post/5349779449/mahr-arabic.

[11] Exodus 22:16–17.

[12] Rabi A. L. Grajevsky, "De quelques réformes des droits de la femme juive à travers les ages," *Revue International de Droit Comparé*, vol. 15, no. 1, 1963, pp. 55–61.

In pre-Islamic Arabia, the *mahr* paid by the groom was fully intended for the father or the guardian of the bride, which necessarily became the subject of a negotiated commercial transaction between the father of the bride and the future husband. While Islam has maintained the principle of the *mahr*, offered by the husband, it has subjected it to a radical modification by considering it a present or a due, not a price. And such due would be accredited to the wife, who becomes its sole owner. In fact, it is a woman's right as stipulated in the following verse: "And give the women their bride wealth as a free gift (*saduqātihinna nihla*)."[13] Ordinarily, such "due" must be paid at the pronouncement of the marriage contract.

In addition to the word *mahr*, the Qur'ān uses several other terms to designate the concept of dowry, including *farīda*, which means an obligation, and *nihla* or *sadāq*, which, respectively, mean a "handsome gift" and a "token of friendship." Whichever term is used, the *mahr* is thus portrayed as a religious obligation and an integral part of the marriage contract. Furthermore, the proceeds of such obligation belong exclusively to the wife for her to do with as she wishes, with no other person, whether a father, a brother, or anyone else, having the right to dispossess her. Apart from the woman's right of sole ownership, the Qur'ān has neither fixed the monetary amounts to be paid nor specified particular traits of such "gifts" in terms of quality or quantity, so that each couple can decide and agree on the specifics and value of the gift according to their means and socioeconomic milieu.

What we must retain here is that the Qur'ān has taken a pre-Islamic discriminatory custom that devalued women and reinstated it within a new framework that values women and grants them rights and obligations. By obliging husbands to offer their brides a gift of cash or kind at the conclusion of the marriage contract and specifying that she is and will remain the sole owner of such a gift, the Qur'ān has radically changed the status of women from the owned property of fathers, brothers, uncles, husbands, and in-laws to dignified and independent legal entities with full rights to own property and to dispose of it as they pleased. And all of this was accomplished in an era of a deeply rooted patriarchal culture, a major victory for women's rights. So, whatever was the value of this gift, high or low, it symbolized a new freedom and respect for women.

---

[13]The Qur'ān 4:4.

Several traditional narrations show that the Prophet has given differ-ent types of guidance to those who came to him concerning the size or value of the *mahr*, depending on the social status and financial means of the inquirer. Thus, the quantity and quality of the *sadāq* ranged from a garden plot, a significant amount of money, a simple metal ring, or even the highly symbolic value of a Qur'ānic verse. This shows that rather than being a trade, or a price, the *mahr* was a good gesture that every groom, depending on his means, would and should do to honor his future wife. By leaving the choice of the monetary value of the *sadāq* to the parties, the Qur'ān acknowledges differential means, regardless of time or place.

It is this philosophy that the first Muslim women had internalized, always ready to battle each time someone tried to bypass Qur'ānic rec-ommendations, in defense of their newly acquired rights. In this regard, a well-known interchange between a woman from the Quraysh tribe and 'Umar Ibn al-Khattāb, as *Khalīfa* at the time, is reported. During a ser-mon in the mosque, 'Umar indicated that the amount of *mahr* should [shall] be limited because of a degree of extravagance and overindul-gence witnessed among the Muslims of the time. Hearing this decision, a woman whose name has not been retained stood up, right in the middle of the congregation gathered in the mosque, questioning 'Umar, with-out hesitation, in these terms: "O 'Umar, you do not have the right to do that! Don't you see what God says in his Holy Qur'ān: 'If you desire to take one wife in place of another, even if you have given to one of them a great sum [*mahr*], take back nothing from it. Would you take it by way of calumny and manifest sin'?"[14] To the woman's challenge and statement, 'Umar responded: "This woman is right, and it is I, 'Umar who is wrong!" The decision he had just made was thus rescinded.[15]

We might want to take a long pause, here, to ponder this narrative, the personality of this woman who does not hesitate to address what appears to be a mixed assembly inside a mosque, the fact that she did not hesitate to debate and correct a decision that had just been taken by the Commander of the Faithful (the Commander-in-Chief) at that time. All of the details of this tale would be unthinkable today, in our Muslim communities, in our modern mosques, sexually hierarchical and morally

---

[14] The Qur'ān 4:20.

[15] There are several versions of this narration, especially the commentary of Ibn Kathīr on verse 20 of *sūrah* 4.

sterile, where women have the allegedly Islamic duty to remain silent, in other words, simply invisible.

A MARITAL RELATIONSHIP FOUNDED ON THE COMMON GOOD

After the initial Qur'ānic warning to men, the Qur'ān, in the same verse, reveals one of the fundamental principles of the marital relationship, symbolized by the concept of the "Common Good" (*ma'rūf*): *wa 'āshirūhunna bil-ma'rūf,* which can be translated as "But consort with them in kindness." The term *ma'rūf* appears more than twenty times in the Qur'ān.[16] It is often interpreted as signifying the good, the correct (reasonable or above board), that which is morally accepted by all, and that which in a given society corresponds with a number of values on which individuals, more or less, agree. This concept also corresponds to what people recognize as a source of benediction for human beings and what logic would recognize as just and in everyone's interest.

The concept of *ma'rūf* also appears to be very close or even equivalent to that of *bonum commune,* a traditional concept that goes back to antiquity (Plato and Aristotle) and the Middle Ages (Thomas Aquinas). In general, it was understood as being the expression of a superior interest, with a nature that is both rational and divine.[17]

This concept, as it appears in this verse, seems to summarize, on its own, the sum of Qur'ānic ethic relative to marital relationships. In his classic *tafsīr,* Ibn Kathīr interprets the term as indicating an aggregate of conduct that men must adopt vis-à-vis their wives. According to Ibn Kathīr, the conducts that form a part of *ma'rūf* and which every husband must observe with his wife include being good and agreeable, speaking kind words, and polishing of physical demeanor and dress. He specifies that, because men are demanding of their wives and appreciate that they adorn themselves for their husbands, husbands must also pay attention to their appearances and spruce up to please their wives.[18] He also cites a

---

[16]The Qur'ān 2:178, 180, 228, 232–234, 236, 241; 3:104, 110, 114; 4:6, 19; 5:6; 7:157; 9:71, 76, 112; 22:41; 31:17.

[17]Denis Müller, "Bien commun, conflits d'intérêts et deliberation éthique," January 2004.

[18] *Tafsīr,* Ibn Kathīr.

Qur'ānic verse, regarding this issue: "[The women] are owed obligations the like of those they owe, in an honorable way."[19]

Ibn 'Abbās, considered as one of the first major commentators of the Qur'ān, has made the following remark to explain this verse: "I like to make myself handsome for my wife as much as I like her making herself beautiful for me."[20] In this sense, beauty does not refer only to the physical appearance; it also embraces a sense of virtue, moral conduct, and "beautiful action" on the part of a spouse toward his/her partner.

Concerning this verse and the concept of *ma'rūf*, the different *tafāsīr* cite many sayings of the Prophet and relate long narratives that describe his exemplary behavior toward his wives. One of the Prophet's most significant sayings on this subject is as follows: "The best among you are those who are the best towards their wives."[21] And he was certainly considered the best of husbands—gallant, sweet, and caring. Never in his life was he heard raising his voice to one of his wives, despite the difficulties they were facing and the trials he had to endure as the Messenger of God.

Thus, the Qur'ān lays down the broad outline of conjugal union, first by providing a vital foundation on which life together must be built. This foundation is symbolized by the Qur'ānic principle of *ma'rūf*, which is repeated several times in the Qur'ān, as an unfailingly reiterated reminder to men. This "*Common Good*" is indispensable in the conjugal union for it to stand solid, despite the vagaries of married life, like a stable foundation of a building that allows the rest of the building to rise, without falling.

The Prophet's tireless support for women continued until the very end, as we see in his Farewell Sermon, when he reminded men of the Qur'ānic principle: "*I urge you to take good care of your wives.*"[22] And the Prophet repeated this recommendation three consecutive times, as if he had feared the future, as if, deep down, he realized that this Islamic principle would be one that Muslims would have the most difficulty understanding, upholding, and practicing. And he was absolutely right. An Egyptian academic has recently written an article on this issue, an article

---

[19] The Qur'ān 2:228.

[20] *Hadīth*, Ibn 'Abbās, cited in Ibn Kathīr's commentary on verse 228 of *sūrah* 2.

[21] *Hadīth*, cited by Ibn Kathīr.

[22] *Hadīth*, cited in Ibn Kathīr's commentary on verse 228 of *sūrah* 2.

whose title sums it all: "O Messenger of God, they have not looked after us, despite your recommendations."[23]

It is disheartening to see how Islamic values such as that of the Common Good are not reflected in the lives of Muslims who read, learn, and listen to the Divine words through the chanting of the Qur'ān, sometimes all day long, without giving importance to the essential principles and moral values that these very words convey. At times, one even gets the impression that the reality of some Muslim societies and communities is in contradiction, at times deeply, to all of these values.

The concept of *ma'rūf* is at the heart of conjugal ethics in the Qur'ān, and it is with reference to such ethics that conjugal union standards of behavior in Islam should be defined, erected, and lived. Thereby, after the mention of *ma'rūf*, the Qur'ān continues, in reference to the *mahr*: "And how can you take it back, when you have lain with one another, and they have made with you a solemn covenant?"[24]

Marriage: An Intimate Union with Much Significance

In the last verse (4:21), we can identify two very important concepts whose profound symbolic significance is immeasurable: *al-ifdhā* (*afdhā ba'dukum ilā ba'dh*) and *al-mīthāq al-ghalīdh*. *Al-ifdhā* refers to the intimate relationship that unites two spouses. Ibn 'Abbās interprets the corresponding expression in the sense of "revealing oneself" or "communicating in secrecy."[25] In other words, it is the intimate loving relationship that unites a couple to the point that their souls reveal one to the other, which results in shared intense proximity of body and of heart. The concept of *al-mīthāq al-ghalīdh* is conventionally treated as a marriage contract (*'aqd*); the expression can in fact be translated literally as a weighty contract not only because it is indeed heavy in terms of responsibility and magnitude but also because this contract is the "solid link" and "firm commitment" that intimately unites the two persons together through life.

The importance of the concept of *al-mīthāq al-ghalīdh* is furthermore confirmed by the fact that it is indeed this very same expression

---

[23] Hiba Izzat Raouf, *lam yastawsū bi-n-nisā khayraan yā rasūlAllāh* (they did not take good care of the women, Oh Prophet), https://islamonline.net/.

[24] The Qur'ān 4:21.

[25] Commentary of Ibn 'Abbās, cited in *Tafsīr Ibn Kathīr*.

that, in the Qur'ān, designates the commitment of Messengers to their Creator.[26] In short, the pact enshrined in married life is as important as the one between the Messengers and the Creator. It is the only contract thus described in the Qur'ān, highlighting the profound interest the Qur'ānic ethic is taking in the marital relationship.

The Qur'ān describes this *Mīthāq*, this "pact," as *ghalidh* (heavy-weight) because it is undeniably a significant moral contract that reflects the commitment of both partners to abide by and respect their joint responsibilities. And when one uses the term "contract," one describes a mutual agreement between two equal partners. This principle also contradicts the practice of forced marriages, deemed proper throughout history and until today, in some parts of the Islamic world and among some Muslim communities in the West where a male relative—father, brother, or uncle—forces a young girl from his family to marry a man he considers suitable, without even bothering to let the young girl know in advance, let alone getting her consent.

An authenticated *hadīth* affirms: "women will be married only with their consent."[27] In the prophetic tradition, one finds numerous accounts whereby the Prophet insists on the consent of the young woman to marry or prohibits coercing of a marriage. And in certain cases, he tried to dissolve a marriage concluded without the prior approval of the woman.

This was the case of Khansa' Bint Khaddām, who had her marriage annulled by the Prophet after having complained about being forced into a marriage by her father. Another account relates the story of a young woman who went to the Prophet to complain that her father married her to a cousin without consulting her. The Prophet gave her the choice to separate from her husband, if that was her desire, or to stay married. In response, the young woman made the following prudent remark: "I finally accepted this marriage but, by complaining, I wanted to show women that our fathers do not have the right to make decisions on our behalf."[28] Thus, at the time of the Revelation, women had understood

---

[26] The Qur'ān 33:7.

[27] *Sahīh al-Bukhāri*, no. 4741. In this *hadīth*, the Prophet also cites the consent of a widow as well as that of a young girl.

[28] Sunan Ibn Mājah: compiled by Muhammad ibn Yazīd Ibn Mājah, this *hadīth* collection, consisting of 4341 *hadīths* in 37 books, is considered to be the last of the six collections of *hadīth*. See https://sunnah.com/ibnmajah.

the new sense accorded by Islam to the marital union. Hence, they insisted on their right to choose their husbands, conforming to the new Qur'ānic commands that came to replace the custom of forced marriages, considered the norm at the time.[29]

In his *Tafsīr*, Ibn Kathīr explains that this *mīthāq ghalīdh* is a bond like no other: "There is no more magnificent or more sublime tie than the bond between two spouses." Ibn Kathīr also indicates that this principle was recognized by scholars of the period to the point of even making it the basis of the marriage contract where the first clause is defined by another Qur'ānic verse: *Imsāk bi ma'rūf aw tasrīh bi ihsān*, which is translated as "keep [her] honorably or release her virtuously."[30] Here, we see another fundamental Qur'ānic principle of conjugal cohabitation. The Qur'ān stipulates that a marriage, according to this reciprocal commitment, can be done only on the bases of this prescription, which commits both partners to live in harmony. In situations where the cohabitation becomes impossible and the disagreement between the two spouses insurmountable, one should know how to separate decently and with mutual leniency and forgiveness. Ultimately, *al-mīthāq al-ghalīdh* is this conjugal framework of mutual generosity but that must be broken with decency and humility when, with time, this *ifdhā* or communion is no longer feasible and the union degenerates into mutual animosity.

There are other concepts in the Qur'ān that describe conjugal unions along the same spirit of reciprocity and interdependence, manifested in terms such as *tarādhī* and *tashāwur*. *Tarādhī* translates as the capacity for joint satisfaction and mutual agreement between the two spouses.[31] The Qur'ānic term *tashāwur* means consultation; here again, the Qur'ān insists on mutual consultation in all of the couple's affairs, including those that might seem most futile or that should normally concern only the women, for example, the weaning of infants, a point raised in the verse. The Qur'ān in fact considers it a decision that should be taken by the two partners.[32]

Agreement and consultation are there as key concepts in the marriage, and one might easily remark that it is the absence of these two

---

[29] See similar accounts in *The encyclopedia of women in Islam*, vol. 1 (Al-Qalam, 2007), p. 153.

[30] The Qur'ān 2:229.

[31] Ibid.:232–233.

[32] Ibid.:233.

components that lead to the failure of many conjugal unions, even if a loving relationship existed between the two. Love alone is not sufficient as, without agreement and consultation, it ends up by being transformed into emotional despotism and winds up destroying everything around it and smoldering itself.

Concerning marriage, the Qur'ān has also made multiple references to the notion of *sakīna*, which can be translated as "serenity," another Qur'ānic concept used in the description of the union that ties a man and a woman.[33] The *Tafsīr* of Ibn 'Ashūr compares this Qur'ānic principle to the joyfulness of the soul.[34] It is in serenity that the union between two beings who love each other can be achieved. *Sakīna* is also the cohabitation of the couple, in dignity and the nobility of calmed emotions. Once again, the love between the spouses should be consolidated by this serenity, this calmness of the soul, to be able to withstand the challenges of living together. Love without serenity can resist neither the time nor the unexpected in life; it ends up perishing of its own passion and lasting only the time of a romance. Love needs serenity to be able to persist and to conquer the heart of its partners, every day of their lives.

Mawadda and *rahma*, which can be translated as "deep love" and "infinite mercy," respectively, are two other principles established in the Qur'ān[35] as the foundation of conjugal union. Conjugal life is described as deep, accompanied by tenderness and compassion—a deep love that the Creator raised in the hearts, a love that is serenely protected by generosity and mutual compassion. These are the sentiments of high moral value that the Creator brought forth in two different hearts, at a moment that is sometimes almost identical, two hearts that can remain sealed forever by this infinite love, imprinted via mutual kindness and tenderness.

It is as if the Qur'ān tried to show that this relationship founded on a deep and generous love becomes, by the force of time and events, a spiritual and physical union so intense that the two partners live in an unfailing symbiotic romance. It is as if one becomes the other, in joy, in pain. The two spouses finish by feeling and sharing the same sentiments, the same ailments, and the same joys. The Qur'ān has alluded to this

---

[33] Ibid. 7:189; 30:21.

[34] Ibn 'Ashūr, op. cit.

[35] The Qur'ān 30:21.

conjugal fusion using a clothing metaphor (*libās*) when it declares: "They are a garment for you and you are a garment for them."[36] Each partner dresses the other, which is similar to the current expression "entering the skin of another," to know them perfectly, to be able to put yourself in their place, in their shoes, and to react, at times, in the same way in front of one of life's ordeals.

One also finds another term to describe marital union, *fadhl*, which can be translated as "generosity." "Forget not bounteousness among yourselves!"[37] The Qur'ān insists on generosity in all that unites the pair: in love, in the giving of oneself, in conduct, even in separation, for better and for worse. Goodness of heart must accompany the two partners every single day, throughout their lives together, so that the children who are raised in such an environment are shaped by kindness and generosity and thereby learn to practice it vis-à-vis others. It is a generosity of heart and spirit that unites the two spouses. In this verse, God exhorts both of them never to forget it: "Forget not bounteousness among yourselves!"[38] In a couple's lifespan, with its multiple constraints, adverse temptations, and its daily routine, how often do we forget the fundamentals of the union with one another? At times, it could be a simple misunderstanding, a crisis, a conflict, for this beautiful relationship to dissipate into forgetfulness and hostility and for the generosity of heart and senses to disappear to make room for bitter resentment and heartbreak, as if nothing "good" had ever happened before.

YOUR WIVES … A "FIELD TO PLOW"?

There are other terms in the Qur'ān that describe the conjugal union, terms whose hidden meaning is yet to be discerned. Before closing this chapter, it would be imperative to cite a verse that has too frequently been interpreted in a most pejorative manner—the one that compares a woman to a *harth*, poorly translated as "field to plow," which, according to some interpretations, grants men the authority and duty to use women as they see fit. From that perspective, the verse has been literally

---

[36] The Qur'ān 2:187.
[37] Ibid.:237.
[38] Ibid.

translated as follows: "Your women are a tilth to you, so go unto your tilth as you will, but send forth for your souls."[39]

To understand the significance of this image, we shall examine the various commentaries and interpretations of this verse with a focus on the context within which it was revealed. While there are several narrations regarding the context, they all agree that it was intended to modify certain customs regarding the marital sexual relationship of the people of Medina (*al-ansār*). According to the account reported by Ibn Kathīr, some Meccan Muslims (*al-muhājirūn*) who married Medina women after the *hijra* reported that these women (of Medina) objected to certain forms of sexual intercourse in which the husband was positioned behind the wife. Indeed, *Ansār* (Medina) women had adopted a Jewish belief that "if the man positioned himself behind the woman at the moment of sexual intercourse, the child born of such a union would be afflicted with strabismus" (be cross-eyed).[40] Hence, the verse was revealed to challenge such a superstitious contention and to reassure Muslims that the position of the man during the act had no consequence for the partners and even less for the children born of such partnership. This does not in the least mean that Islam approved of sodomy, an act that has been forbidden by Islam as attested by numerous *hadīths* that instruct Muslims to avoid sodomy.

Going back to the Qur'ānic expression, "Your women are a tilth to you, so go unto your tilth as you will," the phrase has been interpreted, generally speaking, very literally to denote "a field to cultivate," to signify a permission given to husbands to use their wives as they pleased. To say the least, this type of interpretation is very demeaning to women and breeds a poor image of the sexual act. As discussed previously, the purpose of the Revelation was to liberate the sexual relationship of a couple, not in the least to suggest that women were fields to plow in the literal sense of the word.

Sayyid Hussein Fadlallah, a respected scholar, gives an interesting explanation of the term *harth*. For him, it is an image—the land—that expresses the fertility and richness of life.[41] In fact, the Arabs of the time used the term *harth* very positively to describe anything that was

---

[39] The Qur'ān 2:223.

[40] *Tafsīr*, Ibn Kathīr.

[41] Official site of Sayyid Hussein Fadlallah, http://arabic.bayynat.org.lb.

conceived as fertile, productive, and fruitful. Thus, the word *harth* in the verse should be interpreted in terms of its true significance, "the source of life," and not as "a field to cultivate." In other words, the interpretation of that verse would suggest "your wives are for you a source of life and richness. Go, then to this source as you like (freely)." This interpretation agrees with the philosophy of the Qur'ān regarding women, the notion of the couple, and the harmony of a life together.

The Lag Between the Qur'ānic Ethic and Islamic Law

It is truly regrettable that, generally speaking, Muslim societies do not reflect the Qur'ānic ethic of the conjugal union. The Qur'ānic concepts regarding marriage tend to be absent from the reality of today's Muslims, who use a discourse the contents of which are often alien to Qur'ānic thinking: hegemonic power of the husband; the right of men to decide, to revoke; the right of men to "legitimacy," just because they are men. Too frequently in our Muslim reality, customs have been turned into religious principles that must be observed. A good example is that of obedience (*tā'a*), a notion rehashed in just about every ideological pamphlet directed at women; this so-called principle portrays the absolute submission of a wife to her husband as eminently Islamic, even though we do not find any mention of *tā'a* in the Qur'ānic ethic of marriage.

There are loads of other equally lamentable examples directed at women, including violence against women, the guardianship of women and their treatment as property, the arrogance of husbands who are regarded, according to certain religious interpretations, as proprietors. Such appalling values, incorrectly justified as Islamic, have regrettably been enacted during major crises that have marked the progressive decadence of the Muslim civilization, "values" that are the exact opposite of the spiritual principles described in the Sacred Text of the Qur'ān. It is what some have referred to as the "inversion of values" of Islam through time—where all of the values pronounced by the Qur'ān have been inverted, drained of their senses, distorted, and misguided, but nevertheless used as if they were profoundly Islamic.[42]

---

[42] Eric Geoffroy, *L'islam sera spiritual ou ne sera plus* (PRI, 2009).

Unfortunately, this is what is often reflected in Muslim law (*Fiqh*) regarding the question of marriage and life as a couple. Since its appearance in the ninth century, this Muslim law usurped Qur'ānic values by imposing a restriction on women's rights. Interestingly, by looking through the classic texts of Islamic law, one can appreciate the difficulties that early Muslim jurists experienced, as they tried to understand and confront the enormous advances granted by the Qur'ān to women in particular and the couple in general.

In fact, in all *Fiqh* textbooks, and, with some variation, in more or less all the juridical schools of Muslim law, one finds concepts that exist nowhere in the Qur'ān and hence can be considered "pure products" of the interpretation of the same Muslim jurists pertaining to a given time and a given context. For example, some *Fiqh* manuals, generally speaking, describe marriage (*nikāh*) as a "contract of enjoyment" (*'aqd mut'a*). More precisely, the legal text stipulates that the Creator has established this contract so that the husband may enjoy the body of his wife. In short, the object of such a contract is the sexual satisfaction of the husband.[43] The wife, as described in these marriage "contracts," elaborated by the *Fiqh*, is considered, before all, a body that the man possesses and exploits as he pleases, that is, as long as he has paid the *mahr* and is committed to respecting his "duty of [monetary] support" (*nafaqa*).[44]

Certain legal schools have even compared the marriage contract to a property contract (*tamlīk*), while others have compared it to a sales and purchase contract or agreement.[45] So, for the *Fiqh*, a marriage contract is not the bond that, we have seen in the Qur'ān, passes between two partners, man and woman; it is an accord that passes between two parties, with the husband being the guardian of the wife (*waliyy*) and the object of the contract being the wife and the *mahr*.[46] The obligations of the husband are to support the wife and to pay her a *mahr*; on the other side, she becomes the exclusive "property" of the husband to whom she owes absolute obedience (*tā'a*).

---

[43] Abd Ar-Rahmān al-Jazīrī, *Al'fiqh 'alā al-madhāhib al-arb'a* (Fons Vitae, 2009).

[44] Ibid.

[45] Ibid.

[46] Ibid.

This concept of *tā'a* represents the foundation of marriage and the life of a couple in the Islamic discourse, whether classic or contemporary. It appears that, other than total obedience to her husband, there is no other value in the life of a Muslim woman, because, still according to a certain Islamic discourse, only this notion of obedience would open to the wife the gates of Paradise! Let us remember, once again, that there is no mention in the Qur'ān of the wife obeying her husband. All Qur'ānic concepts regarding marriage even contradict this notion of absolute obedience, as we have seen in the notions of consultation (*tashāwur*) and the reciprocal agreement (*tarādhī*), which are at the heart of the conjugal relationship, along with the other Qur'ānic principles of love, involvement, and mutual compassion.

The supporters of this notion of *tā'a* argue that there are some texts in the prophetic tradition to justify the obedience of the wife to her husband and to try to transform such obedience into a principal value in a conjugal relationship. It is true that there are several *hadīths* that point in that direction, but one must know how to put them back into their specific contexts and to understand the objectives of a *hadīth* rather than stopping with their literal meaning.

One can also legitimately criticize the manner in which this genre of *hadīth* has been manipulated and promoted at the expense of many other *hadīths* that express contrary opinions. Here we should remember the existence of apocryphal sayings (*hadīths* wrongly attributed to the Prophet), especially when their content is opposed to the Qur'ānic ethic and the life and teachings of the Prophet. And this is certainly the case with the two following *hadīths*. Different versions of the first *hadīth* were transmitted; the best known narrates a story attributed to a respected companion of the Prophet, Mu'ādh ibn Jabal, who, having just returned from Syria, prostrated at the feet of the Prophet. The Prophet, astonished at Mu'ād's behavior, someone known to be among the most pious and most learned of his companions, asked him the reason behind such behavior. Mu'ād responded that he had seen the people of Syria prostrating at the feet of their religious leaders, patriarchs and bishops, so he wanted to honor the Prophet in the same manner. The Prophet is reported to having responded, "If I had to order a person to prostrate at the feet of another, I would impose the prostration of a wife at the feet of her husband."[47] First, the content of this *hadīth* is a blatant contradiction to a basic principle of Islam, *tawhīd*, namely that prostration is for God and God alone. The conduct of Mu'ādh Ibn Jabal seems all the more surprising because he was one of the most learned among the companions of the Prophet. It is even to him, according to an authenticated *hadīth*, that the notion of *ijtihād*, the independent intellectual interpretation effort in Islam, is attributed. So, how could a person of Mu'ādh's stature have accepted seeing people prostrating in front of another human being, let alone to admire the behavior to the point of trying to emulate it with the Prophet, when the principle message of Islam was to liberate people from the adoration of idols, be they human or otherwise, and to teach them that adoration is only to God.

What is even more astonishing in this first *hadīth* is the rejoinder attributed to the Prophet, he who never ceased to encourage the autonomy of women and their liberation from cultural oppression and tribal traditions; he who clearly affirmed, to cite one of the authenticated *hadīth*s, "Women are the equals (*shaqā'iq*) of men." Moreover, this *hadīth* about the "prostration of a wife to the husband" has been judged by learned specialists as untrustworthy in terms of its transmission chain (*isnād dha'īf*).[48]

The second *hadīth* of this sort that is attributed to the Prophet is, "The woman has two kinds of protection: the tomb and the husband, and the tomb is better for her."[49] This *hadīth* is even less viable than the preceding one, as it has been acknowledged as apocryphal (*mawdhū'*) by a large number of *'ulamā*. However, it continues to be disseminated even though it blatantly contradicts Qur'ānic principles and the teachings of the Prophet, whose acts and sayings negate such fabrications.

How can he, who strongly supported women's participation in the political engagement represented by the *Bay'a* (the oath of allegiance), who has encouraged women to be present everywhere, in mosques, in social and political gatherings, he who allowed them to claim their rights in terms of economic independence, to be free to act and to speak, how could this same person have simultaneously preferred to see women

---

[47] A *hadīth* reported by At-Tarmidhī (no. 1159) and Ibn Mājah (no. 1852).

[48] See the analysis by Suhayla Zayn al-'Abidīn, member of the International Union of Muslim Scholars, in *Tā'at az-zawj: nadhra tash tashīhiyya* (A Wife's Obedience to Her Husband: A Critical Examination), http://iumsonline.org/en/.

[49] Cited by At-Tabarānī, *Al-mu'jam al-kabīr*, 271/3.

buried in tombs? How could anyone, even for an instant, attribute such insanities to him, he who was never unjust to anyone, whoever he might have been, he who, as the Qur'ān has specified, was the embodiment of moral excellence.[50]

While they have been recognized as inauthentic, there are several apocryphal *hadīths*, all in more or less the same vein, that continue to be included in classical manuals and widely disseminated despite the fact that they are littered with misconceptions about the ideal Muslim woman—obedient, submissive, and fully compliant with the supremacy of men. This is objectionable, particularly when it is done in the name of Islam—to accept and disseminate these kinds of tales that are, over time, regarded as sacred, tales that plant doubt and guilt in the hearts of a large number of Muslims, among whom are practicing Muslim women who feel forced to bow to the dictates imposed by a fundamentally discriminatory ideology that is contrary to the Islamic ethic. It is indeed an obligation to distinguish narratives that are forged by mentalities that are rooted in pre-Islamic customs and regain the values of a spiritual morality as conveyed in the original sources. In this regard, it is undeniably disheartening when eminent scholars such as Ahmad Ibn Hanbal acknowledge that they have retained weak *hadīths* in their compilations due to the influence of the customs of a society.[51]

Concerning marriage norms, it is evident that the early Muslim jurists were strongly marked by the pre-Islamic marriage models, usually conducted under duress (*jabr*); they thus failed to put the Islamic values that abolished coerced marriages in all forms into practice. Marriage, according to the different compilations of the classic *Fiqh* responds to a logic of "domination" and not to that of "equal union," as was advocated by the Qur'ān. In fact, in *Fiqh*, marriage is defined as a contract of exchange, of "rendered services," to make sexual relations lawful. It is noted that, in all legal texts, the primary objective of a marriage is to satiate first and above all the sexual needs of the husband, then childbearing and the preservation of the morals of the community. "Principles" such as absolute obedience, the *waliyy*, understood as a despotic guardian, and the

---

[50] The Qur'ān 68:4.

[51] See, for comparison, the article by Suhayla Zayn al-'Abidīn cited in this chapter.

objectification of women are still used by the *Fiqh*, even though they are completely foreign to Qur'ānic philosophy.[52]

Thus, we are far from the principles that have been stated in the Qur'ān, including the moral commitment between the two spouses, their mutual consent, their consultation, reciprocal love, and tenderness. These notions are progressively disappearing, replaced by concepts that disclose patriarchal cultural imagery of the Muslim jurist of the time, influenced by their own environment. So, even though the Qur'ān describes marriage as a symbol of harmony between two people, the *Fiqh* offers a breeding ground for the contempt of women. There, women are described as sexual objects and not as social beings and individuals in their own right, which is in contradiction to what the Qur'ān has decreed repeatedly, that the essence of the human being, man and woman, lies in their honor and dignity.

With the exception of issues related to the conjugal union, the classic work of Muslim scholars does hold a great spiritual value. Sadly, the Qur'ānic ethic and the teachings of the Prophet seem to have been put aside when it came to the position of women in Islam, thus depriving women of what was granted to them by the Creator. God has honored the human being, man and woman, in imparting them with dignity (*karāma*): "We have indeed honored the children of Adam."[53]

This is particularly the case with Abū Hāmid al-Ghazāli, who, despite his greatness of spirit, his immense knowledge, and his indisputable contribution to Islamic scholarship, remained a hostage of his own sociocultural environment when it came to women—considering marriage a form of institutional slavery in which the woman has no choice other than being the absolute slave of her husband.[54] This is also the case of another learned scholar, Ibn Qāyyim al-Jawziyya, who also compares the wife to a prisoner or a slave living under the guardianship of a husband, described as holding the absolute power. Such a vision reflects the mentality of

---

[52] See, for comparison, Ibn Rushd, *Bidāyat al-mujtahid was hihāyat al-muqtasid*, vol. II, and the author's article on the different legal interpretations on this subject, www.asma-lamrabet.com. The *waliyy* was a subject of dispute among the different legal schools, including the Hanafi school that rejects it.

[53] The Qur'ān 17:70.

[54] Abū Hāmid al-Ghazāli, *ihyā' 'ulūm ad-dīn* (The Revival of the Religious Sciences), "Marriage," *al-maktaba al-arabiyya*, vol. 2, p. 81.

the era in which this eminent scholar lived—the reign of the Mamluk Sultanate in Egypt (1250–1517).[55]

The legal concepts elaborated by a *Fiqh* that was a prisoner of the archaic customs are the product of a long civilizational decadence whose principal ingredients are political despotism and the instrumentalization of religion for the service of governors in need of legitimacy. This image of the wife as a slave of her husband, rooted in the minds of some Muslim scholars, is nothing but a mirror image of many Muslims, men and women—submissive, docile, and obedient to political power. In the name of highly misguided religious principles, a "*Fiqh* of *Ṭā'a*" was produced, a true ideology of submission that would eradicate reflection and the spirit of criticism in order to maintain the confusion between blind obedience to a political leader and that which is due to the Creator.

It is in the name of religion that one makes Muslims believe that women must be absolutely obedient to their husbands who, themselves, must submit to their political or religious leaders, whose powers are often merged deliberately. Ultimately, the question of *ṭā'a* is not only the result of an unalterable patriarchal culture but also the outcome of a hegemonic political culture that starts by exploiting the most vulnerable and the most disadvantaged in a society to better consolidate its power.[56]

CONCLUSION

Through the concepts regarding marriage, the Qur'ān invites us to a true ethic of marital union. The Qur'ānic Word has come to liberate women from the chains of bondage and conjugal despotism. According to the Qur'ān, the union between a man and a woman is not a prison where the woman should submit to all kinds of discrimination; it is, in fact, a place where harmony can be and should be realized. The Revelation started by preserving the property of wives, forbidding their mistreatment, wherever the origin for such treatment might reside, and prohibiting their intimidation. The Qur'ān has imposed common rights and responsibilities on both partners. Given the deep-rooted patriarchy that prevailed in Arabia at the time, it should not come as a surprise to

---

[55] Ibn Qāyyim al-Jawziyya, *I'lām al-muwaqqi'īn*, vol. 2, 1973, p. 106.

[56] Zayd Ibn 'Ali al-Wazīr, *Al-fardiyya* (Al-Manāhil, 2000). A sound analysis of the introduction of autocratic rule in Muslim countries and the impact of such introduction on Islamic thought.

anyone that "cautioning" in the Qur'ān is addressed mostly to men, as we have seen earlier.

The Qur'ān describes the marital union as the home of *ma'rūf*, a home that has no place for brutality, vulgarity, or disrespect. The conjugal relationship is described as an intimate communion of body and soul, an *ifḍā* where each of the two partners relies on the other, in total confidence. Marriage in the Qur'ān is a *mīthāq ghalīḍh*, a solid bond, morally and legally, a place where the commitment of both partners is total and carried out in equal share of mutual acceptance. Such marriage is founded on *al-iḥsān*, excellence, the excellence of union but also of separation, if shared living becomes impossible. The relational reciprocity is made of *tashāwir* (consultation) and *tarāḍhi* (mutual understanding), which, according to the Qur'ān, is a symbol of *sakīna*, a delicate serenity where each finds in the other the contentment of his or her soul. It is the place where love is always protected by profound bounty, by the peace of the soul, by the respect of one another, and by pardon of misconduct that might have been committed by the other. In short, it is the abode of *mawadda* and *rahma*. It is the conjugal ethic of which the Qur'ān speaks, the ethic that covers both partners in the same *libās* (the same garment), just like a shared second skin.

Naturally, some are bound to say that such a vision is idealistic and cannot exist in the reality that millions of couples live, with tears, daily disappointments, and accumulated sufferance, a reality where spirituality becomes increasingly difficult given what couples must live through and endure. While this is indeed a reasonable conclusion, we should keep in mind that the Qur'ān is, above all, a spiritual message that describes an "ideal" existence that Muslims should strive to live by, to emulate. For Muslim women and men, the Qur'ān should be the essential reference to which one must know how to return each time the routine, the passage of time, and the daily discomforts threaten to take over and each time injustice is committed, and sometimes even justified, using what people might believe to be religious principles. There are no principles in the Qur'ān that justify injustice and discrimination. None. And this remains true regardless of the rationale used.

Sadly, the first cultural revolution of Islam in favor of women—the Qur'ānic ethic of the conjugal union—was virtually suffocated in its cradle, confined to a corner of history, and supplanted by interpretations that took no heed of the Qur'ānic ethic that banned archaic traditions and liberated women as well as men through the humanization of the institution of marriage. Such discriminatory "religious" ideology remains a barrier to the implementation of the Qur'ānic morality regarding the conjugal union and family affairs.

CHAPTER 10

The Principles of Divorce in the Qur'ān

As opposed to Christianity,[1] divorce is permitted in Islam, because marriage is not regarded as a sacrament but as a contract that can be severed. So while in Christianity the conjugal union is unbreakable, from the very beginning, Islam has established principles for the legislation of divorce. Divorce existed in the pre-Islamic Arab society, but only as the exclusive right of husbands who were free to "repudiate" their wives any time they wished and in any way they saw fit. Despite the pioneering Qur'ānic directions, we remain unable to protect women from this abusive custom—repudiation—that embodies one of the most malicious forms of discrimination against Muslim women today.

It is shocking to see the magnitude of the ideological gap between the Qur'ānic prescriptions concerning divorce and the provisions of the Islamic law (*Fiqh*) that institutionalized a set of bylaws (*ahkām*) that benefit husbands and constrain wives. Through these *ahkām*, the *Fiqh* deprives wives of the rights that had been granted to them by the Qur'ān by downgrading these given rights to a number of minor moral obligations that completely depend on arbitrary will and whims, very often those of their husbands.

---

[1] This is in reference to Orthodox Christianity.

© The Author(s) 2018
A. Lamrabet, *Women and Men in the Qur'ān*,
https://doi.org/10.1007/978-3-319-78741-1_10

What Does the Qur'ān Say on the Topic of Divorce?

It is very important that we clarify, from the start, that while the Qur'ān certainly speaks about divorce (*talāq*), it never discusses repudiation, as has been articulated not only in numerous translations of the Qur'ān but also in certain legal understandings of the notion of divorce in Islam.

The Arabic term *talāq* signifies the "breakup of bond," in this case, the marriage bond. In the Qur'ānic context of the conjugal union, *talāq* corresponds to a rupture of the marriage contract, as determined by one or both of the partners, as is the case in divorce by mutual consent. Nowhere in the Qur'ān does one find any reference to the equivalence of the English term "repudiation," especially its pejorative connotation, which implies the *sine die* (for an indefinite period) revocation of a wife by a husband who alone holds the absolute power to break the marriage bond. According to the Qur'ān, divorce is a right that can be exercised by a man or a woman. This Qur'ānic reality is contrary to the established practice found in numerous Islamic legislations, which are much more in line with the norms of customary law (*'urf*) than they are with Qur'ānic prescriptions.[2]

Several passages in the Qur'ān speak of different types of divorce according to different situations. One can nevertheless distinguish among three scenarios that seem to sum up the Qur'ānic stance on divorce.

Divorce by Mutual Consent

Divorce by mutual consent is described in two verses in the Qur'ān:

> And if you fear a breach between the two, then appoint an arbiter from his people and an arbiter from her people. If they desire reconciliation, God will bring about agreement between them. Truly, God is Knowing, Aware.[3]

> If the two separate, God will enrich both out of His abundance, and God is All-Encompassing, Wise.[4]

---

[2] The 2004 family code in Morocco, which resulted from a rereading of the Qur'ān, describes divorce as breaking the marriage contract, exercised by both the husband and the wife, according to their conditions and subject to the discretion of a judge.

[3] The Qur'ān 4:35.

[4] Ibid.:130.

These two verses summarize the essence of the Qur'ānic philosophy relative to the conjugal relationship that is, above all, considered to be founded on harmony and mutual understanding. Starting from that principle, the Qur'ān considers it to be better for the couple to separate in cases in which there are profound misunderstandings or irreconcilable differences that risk destabilizing the established mutual agreement. We see many examples of this today—destabilized marriages that continue to exist because of social, cultural, or religious constraints, despite the fact that they have been transformed into hotbeds of violence and reciprocal abuse, not to mention destructive psychological dramas with strong negative impacts on the household, especially the children for whom, almost invariably, such violence leaves deep and permanent scars.

At the same time, a resolution to divorce should not be taken lightly in Islam and should be resorted to only as a last recourse, in cases of enduring, serious conjugal problems. However, before a decision of definitive separation is made, it is strongly advised that there be earnest attempts at reconciliation. The Qur'ān steadfastly attempts to persuade couples against hasty decisions. In this regard, the Qur'ān tries to stop both men and women from making injudicious decisions, as we see in the following verses:

> And consort with them in a kind and honorable way; for if you dislike them, it may be that you dislike a thing in which God has placed much good.[5]

> If a wife fears animosity or desertion from her husband, there is no blame upon them should they come to an accord, for an accord is better. Souls are prone to avarice, but if you are virtuous and reverent, surely God is aware of whatsoever you do.[6]

Moreover, a *hadīth* indicates the limits within which divorce is permitted: "Divorce is the one thing that is permitted which God, nevertheless, detests the most." It is in this sense that the first verse cited earlier (4:35) advocates, in cases of "conflict" or risk of deep disagreement between the spouses, the involvement of a referee of the family of the husband and another of the family of the wife. Such mediation, recommended by the Qur'ān, aims at giving each spouse enough time to thoroughly

[5] The Qur'ān 4:19.
[6] Ibid.:128.

rethink the logic for the separation and to reflect upon the consequences of divorce. Hence, the two mediators should first focus, as much as possible, on the likelihood of reconciliation and search for a potential peaceful resolution of the issues posed by each of the two partners. If they succeed in soothing the conflict between the two, this will facilitate the resumption of the couple's cohabitation.

Referring back, once again, to the same verse (4:35), we can recognize, through the commentary of Ibn Kathīr, how well early Muslims comprehended the meaning of the condition of "conflict" that the Qur'ān posed. In fact, facing a conflict between the two spouses, the 'ulamā of the time period stipulated that, initially, under the order of the governor, the two partners should be placed in a safe haven to prevent acts of abuse from either side. Next, the governor should call for family mediation, as stipulated in the Qur'ān. Ibn Kathīr moreover states that, according to the 'ulamā, after deliberation, it was up to the mediators and the judge to determine which solution—separation, divorce, or reconciliation—would be best.[7] It is therefore entirely valid, in connection with this verse, to speak of a "judicial divorce for discord." In fact, in cases of disagreement between the spouses, one or the other or both may seek divorce through this very process.

For centuries, this principle of judicial divorce remained underrated by most Islamic legislators and legislations. It was not until recently, mainly in Morocco, that this procedure, which was laid down by the Qur'ān and is consistent with international laws on divorce, was adopted.

This procedure can be considered one of the outstanding innovations of the new code in Morocco and an important achievement for equality between men and women before the law, especially because it "places women at the same level of competence as men in the dissolution of a marriage, and thus breaks away from the previous situation governed by the former Moudawana,[8] whereby a decision concerning a woman's wish

---

[7] *Tafsīr Ibn Kathīr*, commentary 4:35.

[8] The Moroccan Family Code (Moudawana) of February 5, 2004, was "drafted in conformity with Islam's tolerant rules and exemplary purposes while providing balanced, fair and pragmatic solutions resulting from enlightened open ijtihad (juridical reasoning). This code further stipulates that human and citizenship rights are accorded to all Moroccans, women and men equally, in respect of the holy divine religious references." Gender equality and Women's Empowerment, The Moroccan Family Code (Moudawana), The Global Human Rights Education and Training Centre (HREA), February 5, 2004.

to separate from her husband remained suspended for a long time, at the sole discretion of the husband."[9]

In parallel with the first verse that permits divorce at the request of the two partners, the second verse establishes the foundations of the divorce by mutual consent: "And if you fear a breach between the two, then appoint an arbiter from his people and an arbiter from her people. If they desire reconciliation, God will bring about agreement between them. Truly, God is Knowing, Aware" (4:35).

The remarkable realism of Islam—after all avenues for dialogue have been exhausted and all attempts for mediation and reconciliation have proven futile—is demonstrated by the open admission that, in such circumstances, divorce is the only viable option. In that case, it can be initiated by either partner following a procedure that the Qur'ān portrayed with great simplicity and insight. In fact, the verse could not have been any clearer, describing the divorce by mutual consent as being the best way of parting, in kindness and composure.

One cannot but be puzzled when we compare this Qur'ānic text that describes with such fluidity the deliberate choice of two spouses to separate, without coercion, with the everyday reality of the divorce of Muslim couples, usually shrouded in endless conflict and tears, not to mention the hellish legal mesh. The situation is particularly tragic for women, especially when their husbands refuse the peaceful separation by mutual consent, in preference of repudiation, regarded as an honorable way of asserting his male authority, by humiliating his divorced wife.

The sequel of the verse is also very significant. After the proposition of separation as an option is offered to the two partners, the Qur'ān declares: "God will enrich both out of His abundance" (4:130), soothing words to the couple who have decided to divorce since, whether we like it or not, the separation is always painful and does often leave behind deep scars in the heart. In his infinite wisdom, God dresses the wounds of the heart by giving hope for a better fate, better day, and a better future life for both parties. The verse is to moderate the sorrows and resentment that any separation generates and to offer hope and trust in a better tomorrow.

Divorce, as presented in this verse, forces us to consider what a grueling experience separation is likely to be, but to recognize, whatever

[9]Aïcha El Hajjami, *Le Code de la famille à l'épreuve de la pratique judiciaire*, *Service de cooperation et d'action culturelle* (The French Embassy, Morocco, 2009), p. 54.

the particular situation might entail, that wisdom resides in the capacity to make allowances, on both sides, in humility, in peace, and with mutual respect of each other. To separate and depart but, at the same time, keep in one's heart souvenirs of a past common life, with its good and bad, and maintain the links that must endure, especially when the divorcing couple have children in common, and certainly, as the verse says, to place one's confidence in Providence, and draw strength in the certainty of a better life to come. The spiritual message of Islam continues to bid humans to be indulgent vis-à-vis each other, whatever the circumstances might be, as one can see in the other verse relative to divorce: "Forget not bounteousness among yourselves."[10] It is this mutual indulgence, full of humanity and goodwill, that we must keep in mind and know how to apply to the reality of our lives. This verse on divorce by mutual consent is certainly succinct, simple, but also powerful in the strength of its message and the depth of its wisdom—part if you must but remain humble and courteous toward your spouse and always remember the mutual indulgence that you owe to each other.

DIVORCE AT THE REQUEST OF THE HUSBAND

The second form of divorce is one that is carried out at the request of the husband. The procedure is described in detail in the following verses:

O Prophet! When you divorce your wives, divorce them for the waiting period and count well the waiting period, and reverence your Lord. Expel them not from their houses; nor shall they depart, unless they commit a flagrant indecency.[11] These are the limits set by God; and whosoever transgresses the limits set by God has surely wronged himself. Thou knowest not: perhaps God will bring something to pass thereafter.

So, when they have fulfilled their term, take them back in an honorable way (*ma'rūf*) or separate from them in an honorable way [*ma'rūf*]. And call two just persons among yourselves to witness and uphold the testimony for God.[12]

---

[10] The Qur'ān 2:237.

[11] *Fāhisha mubayyina*: adultery or some other reprehensible act.

[12] The Qur'ān 65:1–2. In fact, the first eight verses of this surah, called *al-Talāq* (divorce), composed of twelve verses, deal directly with the question of divorce.

According to most classic commentators of the Qur'ān, while the first recommendation is made to the Prophet, it also addresses all men.[13] And one can deduce from the same verse that this prescription applies equally to the Prophet in his role of supreme representative of the community of believers, as well as all men, without the slightest differentiation among them in terms of these principles.

Most of the classic commentaries relate accounts that reveal the extreme casualness with which men at the time of revelation employed divorce[14] and viewed it as a male entitlement. And they exercised such prerogative to repudiate their wives orally, as and when they pleased, with a simple formula such as the infamous "you are divorced" (*antī tāliq*). According to the Islamic jurisprudence that remains in force in the majority of Muslim countries, this formula, repeated by the husband three consecutive times, marks a definitive divorce.

We must strongly emphasize here that, as such, this divorce "practice" simply does not exist in the Qur'ān or the *hadīth*. Classic commentaries regarding this verse report the anger of the Prophet when someone related to him that a Muslim man had repudiated his wife through the simple enunciation of the aforementioned formula, *antī tāliq*, repeated three times. The Prophet is reported to have responded in bitterness and disappointment: "You alter the content of the Book of Allah while I am still amongst you!"[15] In fact, the Qur'ān is very clear, as evidenced in the cited verse—a divorce solicited by a husband must respect three stages before it becomes legally valid.

Stage One: "When you divorce your wives, divorce them for the waiting period and count well the waiting period, and reverence your Lord." At this stage, the husband who is the "claimant" of the divorce may initiate the process, but in total respect of a "period" (*'idda*), which national and international legislations refer to as the "period of waiting."[16] According to the majority of exegeses, this waiting is for a period of three months to establish whether the woman is pregnant, essential

---

[13] Cf. *Tafsīr* of Zamakhsharī, commentary on these verses.

[14] Ibid.

[15] A *hadīth* reported by Zamakhsharī, in his commentary on the verse.

[16] According to French jurisdiction, the law had instituted a waiting period of 300 days (to avoid possible paternity conflicts) during which the divorced wife could not contract a new marriage. This provision was repealed by law No. 2004-439 of May 26, 2004.

for the determination of the paternity of a child born. Once this period has passed, the divorce becomes definitive and the woman may remarry.

Stage Two: "Expel them not from their houses; nor shall they depart, unless they commit a flagrant indecency. These are the limits set by God; and whosoever transgresses the limits set by God has surely wronged himself. Thou knowest not: perhaps God will bring something to pass thereafter." During this stage of divorce proceedings, the husband is prohibited from dismissing the wife from the matrimonial residence.

Unfortunately, this is a condition that is frequently violated in Muslim societies nowadays; the husband accords himself the right, often with the society's sanction, to chase the wife away from the conjugal home for the smallest transgression in the belief that, from the moment he decides to divorce, his wife must leave the "premises" instantly (*illico presto*). Countless times, our society witnesses agonies that are suffered by women, forcibly dislodged from their homes, often under the terrified gaze of their children, and finding themselves on the street, without shelter. What is even worse is that such abuse is often legitimized by cultural traditions that, ironically, accuse the victims of having brought it upon themselves. Most of them end up going back to their families, who are at times not very welcoming, especially if the parents are deceased. Those without families, even unwelcoming ones, are left on the street, pushed to survive by begging or even prostitution.

The Qur'ānic verse stipulates the exact opposite of this abusive conduct, urging Muslim men not to chase away their wives unless they have committed a voluntary act of notorious shame (*fāhisha mubayyina*), which most exegeses interpret as adultery. So, apart from *proven* adultery (in compliance with the stipulations of testimony), a husband has no right to force his wife to leave the family residence.

In fact, a closer examination of this verse reveals that the Qur'ān uses the feminine form to speak of "their homes" (*buyūtihinna*), signifying the homes of the women, not the "conjugal home" shared by both partners or the home that is specifically the husband's. With this small detail, feminizing the language of the ownership of the dwelling (*buyūtihinna*), the Qur'ān makes it clear that the conjugal home is principally the abode of the wife—her shelter.[17] This close attention that the Qur'ān pays to the wife, considering her, before all, the owner of the dwelling,

---

[17] Hanān Laham, *Adhwā' hawla sūrat at-talāq* (Dār al-hanān, 2008).

even if it belongs, in terms of physical ownership, to the husband, is not fortuitous. In fact, apart from the few cases where both partners share property rights, it is usually the husband who provides housing, rental or purchased and owned. In addition to the moral vision of the Qur'ān, according the wife primary right to the joint residence, the Qur'ān acknowledges the wife's important contributions, moral and physical, to the building and raising of the family.

Looking at the division of labor within most households in just about every society, women are the ones who carry the bulk if not the totality of domestic responsibilities: cleaning, cooking, caring for the children, and providing them with all the support they need, physical and emotional. And since domestic work is unpaid labor, it is rarely taken into account.[18] This includes households where both partners are fully employed since, most of the time, the wives are the ones who carry the burdens of a "second shift," rushing home at the end of a full workday to do or to finish what could not be done or completed in the early morning hours before leaving for work. Such work, no matter the number of hours or the quality of contribution, essential for the sustainability of normalcy of family life, is not taken into account in the economic life of societies and is always considered, even in advanced industrial countries, as unproductive labor.[19]

This Qur'ānic assertion not to chase women from "their homes" goes beyond a symbol; it testifies to the Qur'ān's recognition of the central role a wife plays in the context of the family in terms of the management of the conjugal home, the care for the children, and the rearing of a family. One also notes in this second stage that the Qur'ān is trying to suspend the finality of a divorce via a "period of waiting," which in addition to the verification of pregnancy allows the couple to think over the decision to divorce and to reflect upon the future consequences of their lives as a couple and as a family, especially in the case of the presence of children. This is what should be understood by "Thou knowest not: perhaps God will bring something to pass thereafter." This statement highlights the importance of the distance between the time of the conflict and the

---

[18] "Partage des tâches: chantier en cours," *Le Monde*, June 28, 2011. Women in France continue to do 80% of the domestic work.

[19] With the exception of Scandinavian countries where genuine social policies, such as paid paternity leave and the institutionalization of nurseries in workplaces, have been established to promote a balanced sharing of parenthood.

final decision of divorce, which, as we have seen, should be taken as a last resort.

Stage Three: "So, when they have fulfilled their term, take them back in an honorable way (*ma'rūf*) or separate from them in an honorable way [*ma'rūf*]. And call two just persons among yourselves to witness and uphold the testimony for God." Once the waiting period has passed, the husband, after serious consideration and reflection, decides whether reconciliation is possible "take them back in an honorable way," or, given that a life together is no longer feasible, because of irreconcilable differences, to separate from his spouse, guided by the protocol specified by the Qur'ān, "or separate from them in an honorable way [*ma'rūf*]."

Whether the decision is to maintain the marriage or to proceed to a final divorce, the Qur'ān leaves it entirely in the hands of the two partners. However, the Qur'ān insists that, whatever the decision might be, the process must be conducted with an eye to excellence, decorum, propriety, and a sense of fairness and justice, all summed up in the notion of *ma'rūf*, which should accompany the interaction of a couple whether they decide to stay together or move apart.

It is, relatively speaking, easy to understand why reconciliation should be conducted according to the ethical criteria of *ma'rūf*. What is much more difficult for many Muslims and non-Muslims to appreciate is the need to adhere to the same type of conduct during separation and divorce. As we have seen, the Qur'ān does not in the least differentiate between these two situations in terms of appropriate conduct. For the Qur'ān, believers should respect this basic principle of decorum, in reconciliation as in separation. Such dignified conduct, regardless of the particular situation or conclusion, is an excellent indicator of a genuine spirituality and unwavering faith.

Respecting the rules of *ma'rūf* during separation, as made very clear in the cited verse of the Qur'ān, starts with not chasing a wife away from her conjugal home. It also entails giving women all the rights that are due to them, including the right to human dignity, respect, a decent life, the assurance of adequate alimony and child support, and the right to keep her children. The welfare of the children and the maintenance of good relationships come under what the Qur'ān has referred to in this verse as the "Common Good."

Regarding alimony, the Qur'ān has prompted men to award divorced woman their due: "And for divorced women an honorable provision—an obligation upon the reverent."[20] It is very important to note that such provision is cited in the Qur'ān as a *right* that must be accorded to divorced wives, especially when it is the husband who is asking for a divorce, without good cause. This is a sort of consolation gift, accorded to the wife by the husband, justified by the injuries suffered by the wife, divorced for no good reason, at the decision of the husband.

Over fourteen centuries ago, the Qur'ānic revelation described divorce in general and that solicited by the husband in particular as a "peaceful divorce," or, using a current term, "civilized divorce." Indeed, the Qur'ān, specifically in this verse, urges men, to whom it is first addressed, to always use the rules of decorum vis-à-vis their wives, whatever the situation or the outcome might be—reconciliation or divorce.

It is true that the circumstances of reconciliation are very different from those of separation, which is always difficult to support, especially when one partner, usually the wife, is paying a high moral price. Nevertheless, the Qur'ān insists on the concept of *ma'rūf*, which is one of the foundations of the Islamic ethic, which permits one to put it all, especially the separation, into perspective. *Ma'rūf* as an ethic of good conduct becomes a condition and prerequisite to all divorce procedures, especially when it is done at the demand of the husband.

It is almost pointless, at this point, to summon up the manner in which most modern divorces transpire, starting with the great suffering of the women who are usually the ones subjected to the divorce and the accompanying humiliation but also the endless conflicts that might go on for years and the harmful consequences, especially for the children. Often, people separate in hatred, mutual contempt, resentment, and a virtual denial of a recent shared history. The Islamic ethic reminds us, precisely, that such mutual violence between partners, during separation and divorce procedures, is deleterious for the future of the two partners and is the exact opposite of what *ma'rūf* stands and calls for.

Thus, the Qur'ān incites the partners to try to find a common ground, marked by *ma'rūf*, which would assist each partner to dispose of the resentments generated by their respective egos. This Qur'ānic verse on divorce concludes by another fundamental Islamic principle that of testimony: "take them back in an honorable way (*ma'rūf*) or separate from them in an honorable way. … And call two just persons among

[20] The Qur'ān 2:241.

yourselves to witness and uphold the testimony for God." Once again, the Qur'ān is very clear in terms of the importance of testimony by advocating the settlement of marital disputes in the presence of witnesses. This testimony symbolizes the engagement of each partner, especially the one responsible for initiating the divorce procedures, most often the husband, in front of upright third parties, trustworthy and competent in the matter.

This type of witnessing can be equivalent to a judicial divorce, established in court, in front of a tribunal or a judge. And while this verse touches on a very important point, unfortunately, in the majority of divorces in Islamic societies, one has never given any consideration to this principle, highly avant-garde for its time, which presupposes the "legalization" of reconciliation or divorce before witnesses.

Islamic jurisprudence has always given the Muslim man the right to divorce, in the sense of repudiating his wife, without any justification, let alone, in front of witnesses. The husband was and still is the one who is authorized by law to keep or repudiate his wife. This manner of proceeding could result in situations in which a wife could be living in an unclear marital status for quite a long time. This verse is nevertheless very significant in according prime importance to witnesses (testimony), in other words, the formalization of such an event, be it the resumption of conjugal life or a final decision of divorce.

Indeed, this testimony helps to prevent abuse, especially that of men. It could, however, also be the wives who might be the abusers of their spouses, especially in our modern times. The legalization of such acts means contributing to a greater transparency and the reinforcement of the principles of law and justice for each of the two partners. The presence of witnesses creates a climate of trust that is necessary for the resolution of problems raised by the dissolution of the marriage, while putting each of the two partners before his or her commitments and responsibilities. Neither the classic exegesis nor the Islamic jurisprudence has given this Qur'ānic verse the importance it merits. Ibn Kathīr denounces this breach and insists on the importance of witnesses as he reports the view of some Muslim scholars of the first generation who affirmed the invalidity of reconciliation or a divorce, without the presence of witnesses, in accordance with the directives of the Qur'ān stating that witnesses must be fair and impartial.[21]

---

[21] Cf. *Tafsīr Ibn Kathīr*, commentaries on the first verses of *sūrah* 65.

We can therefore conclude that, contrary to the practice that, unfortunately, is still widely recognized in the lands of Islam, the husband does not have an absolute and arbitrary right to divorce. The verse that addresses divorce at the request of the husband states several principles in an utmost strict, rigorous, and pedagogic tone: the respect of a period of waiting to reflect on what might have happened or likely to happen; the prohibition of the expulsion of the wife from her conjugal home; the importance of the ethic of excellence and fairness, whether in reconciliation or divorce; and the necessity of legalizing all of these actions and decisions in front of competent witnesses. These are the fundamental elements that were stipulated by the Qur'ān over fourteen centuries ago, in cases where the divorce is done at the request of the husband. Sadly, these guidelines are rarely included in the legislations in force in Muslim countries.[22]

DIVORCE AT THE REQUEST OF THE WIFE

The third type of divorce is that requested by the wife (*khul'*). The Qur'ān speaks of it in the following verse:

> Divorce is twice; then keep [her] honorably, or release [her] virtuously. It is not lawful for you to take aught from what you have given [your wives], except that the two should fear that they would not uphold the limits set by God. So if you fear that they will not uphold the limits set by God [the wife initiates the divorce], there is no blame upon the two in what she may give in ransom. These are the limits set by God; so transgress not against them. And whoever transgresses against the limits set by God, it is they who are the wrongdoers.[23]

According to the exegeses, this verse was revealed in order to end pagan practices that gave the husband the right to repudiate his wife or to bring her back as often as he desired. According to Ibn Kathīr, before the advent of Islam, the husband could repudiate and then take back his wife as often as a hundred times.[24] The revelation of this verse aimed

---

[22] With the exception of Tunisian legislation and the new reform in Morocco, both of which show real progress; however, they have not yet been implemented on the ground.

[23] The Qur'ān 2:229.

[24] *Tafsīr Ibn Kathīr*, commentary on the verse.

at limiting divorce to two times by decreeing the impossibility of taking a wife back for a third time, except in the case where she might have remarried, after her divorce from her first husband, and then got divorced from her second husband.

Here, we see how the Qur'ān defines the boundaries of an everyday infringement, practiced by the men who believed that women were their private property and that they had all the rights freely to dispose of these creatures whom they considered of a lower order, created solely for their well-being on earth. The closing of this verse indicates the possibility for the wife to ask for divorce via the payment of a compensation to the husband (*fīmā iftadat bihi*), without specifying in the least the reason for the divorce or the type or amount of compensation. The divorce in return for compensation—called *khul'* in the terminology of *Fiqh*—is one of the procedures that are available to wives. While it is much less practiced in Muslim societies, this possibility has been recognized, from the beginning, in Islamic jurisprudence. The Arabic term *khul'* comes from the verb *khala'a*, which means repeal or undo. This form of divorce is thus a legal process that allows a wife to "repeal" the marriage bond.

We must emphasize, however, that the modalities of this process in Islamic law have not always been consistent with the Qur'ānic ethic. Indeed, this "right" of the wife has often been used as a way of pressuring women in order to "refund" the *mahr*, which contradicts the verse and the egalitarian spirit of divorce according to the Qur'ān. The commentary of Ibn Kathīr gives a succinct clarification of this divorce procedure initiated by the wife: "If the wife detests her husband and can no longer support cohabitation, she should give back the material gift he had given her at the marriage contract."[25]

It should be noted that the term *khul'* does not appear in the Qur'ān. When one talks of the divorce possibility for the benefit of the wife, the expression used in the Qur'ān is *fīmā iftadat bihi*, which literally means "whatever she can afford to compensate the husband." Once again, the Qur'ān does not specify the value, the rules, or the nature of such compensation—is it material or moral?

A famous *hadīth* of the Prophet, reported by al-Bukhārī and other scholars, interprets the Islamic philosophy and the objective of this type of divorce. It is reported that a woman—the wife of Thābit Ibn

[25] Ibid.

Kays—came to the Prophet to say that while she had nothing to com-plain about concerning her husband, neither morally nor religiously, she no longer desired to stay in the marriage, in fear of committing a trans-gression. The Prophet asked her if she accepted to return to her husband the orchard he had given her at the time of marriage, as a wedding gift. She accepted to do so. Thus, this divorce became the first case example of a divorce through compensation in Islam.[26]

One cannot but marvel at the ease with which the Prophet addressed this issue. With his usual discretion and diplomacy, the Prophet tried to satisfy both parties so that the separation is as easy to tolerate as possi-ble for both partners, financially and morally. In light of this verse and the follow-up *hadīth*, we observe that Islam authorizes women to divorce without having to provide detailed explanation or justification. However, in a situation in which the husband did not seem to have any desire to end the marriage, but the wife wanted "out," it would be only "fair" for the wife, according to her means, to compensate him for the breach of the marriage bond, a breach that is likely to have moral and financial consequences. Before Islam, the question of a wife being able to "buy out" her freedom from the husband, according to her means, to be released of a marriage that was no longer tolerable, simply did not exist. Unless the husband wished otherwise, a woman was doomed to a mar-riage, no matter how intolerable or abusive it was or had become, until the day she died.

In his treatise on *Fiqh*, in the chapter that deals with *khul'*, Ibn Rushd,[27] the most celebrated jurist and scholar, specifies that most classic jurists affirm that it is prohibited for the husband to accept a

---

[26] *Hadīth* reported in *Saḥīḥ al-Bukhārī*, vol. 9, p. 352, and in the Collection of An-Nasā'ī, vol. 6, p. 169. An-Nasā'ī's collection is considered to have the fewest weak *hadiths* after the two *Saḥīḥ al-Bukhārī*.

[27] Known in the West as Averroes, Ibn Rushd (1126–1198; born in Cordoba, died in Marrakech) was an influential philosopher who at "the request of the Almohad caliph Abu Ya'qub Yusuf ... produced a series of summaries and commentaries on most of Aristotle's works ... and on Plato's Republic, which exerted considerable influence in both the Islamic world and Europe for centuries. ... He wrote the *Decisive Treatise on the Agreement Between Religious Law and Philosophy (Faṣl al-Maḳāl), Examination of the Methods of Proof Concerning the Doctrines of Religion (Kashf al-Manāhij)*, and *The Incoherence of the Incoherence (Tahāfut al-Tahāfut)*, all in defense of the philosophical study of religion against the theologians." Averroes, Muslim Philosopher, Editors of the Encyclopedia Britannica, June 21, 2002.

"compensation" higher than what he had offered his wife at the time of marriage. In addition, the amount of the compensation should be left to the discretion of the wife based on her means, something that only she can appraise. On the basis of the *hadīth* cited previously, Ibn Rushd further specifies that any exaggerated claim by the husband would be an abuse akin to plunder.[28] Ibn Rushd also mentions that according to certain Muslim scholars who are opposed to any reclamation of the marriage gift or *mahr*, even in the case of a divorce by *khul'*, insofar as it is prohibited by other verses, this even applies to the smallest portion of the goods offered to the wife as a nuptial gift.[29]

Ibn Rushd concluded his exposé on divorce by *khul'* saying: "divorce (*talāq*) is guaranteed to a man if he feels a dislike for his wife; in the same way, the *khul'* guaranteed to a woman if she feels a dislike for her husband."[30] What stands out in cases of a divorce requested by the wife is that the wife does not owe her husband any compensation if he has subjected her to any prior suffering or injury.

This compensation has to be within the limits of the means of the wife and according to the *hadīth* of the Prophet must correspond, more or less, to the amount of the *mahr*, while taking into consideration the financial situation of the wife.[31] So, when we go back to the principles found in the Qur'ān as well as the *hadīth*, concerning divorce by compensation, we realize that the woman, herself, can take the initiative to break the bond of marriage from the moment she can no longer tolerate life as a couple, without the husband having committed mistakes or breaches of his obligations as a husband. Thus, both the man and the woman have the same privilege in terms of divorce.

The compensation in a divorce initiated by the woman is the mirror image of the "consolation gift" in cases in which the divorce is initiated by the husband. And this "consolation gift" in both the first and second cases remains subject to the same Qur'ānic logic: To amend the damage

---

[28] Ibn Rushd, op. cit., p. 112.

[29] This is particularly the view of Abū Bakr ibn 'Abd Allāh al-Māzini, cf. supra, p. 111.

[30] Ibid., p. 113.

[31] The nature and amount of the compensation have generated a number of debates among Muslim jurists and scholars. For example, in the Māliki school of jurisprudence, the sum that the wife must pay her husband is not specified. Nevertheless, it is advisable that it would be the equivalent of the amount of *mahr*; others insist that the compensation is not important and that the divorce can take place without a return.

suffered by the party that did not intend to divorce was not at fault and, on the contrary, might have even wanted to continue life as a couple.

Unfortunately, Muslim jurisprudence does not in the least reflect this egalitarian principle; in the vast majority of *Fiqh* treaties, we see that a divorce initiated by the wife is necessarily accompanied by the financial compensation due to the husband, even though, in the divorce solicited by the husband, the restitution of the wife remains of the order of discretionary, not compulsory.

At present, there is a big difference between this divorce model and the accepted practices and legal provisions in most Islamic countries. The *khul'* is drained of its principles to the point where the wife might find herself totally trapped, with the husband refusing to accept the divorce or to give her child support, and feeling forced to relinquish all her rights in order to gain her freedom, ethically unacceptable in view of the Qur'ānic verses that evoke the rights of women in divorce cases. In short, the Qur'ān puts both partners on an equal footing with regard to dissolving a marriage, regardless of the different scenarios.

What Does Islamic Jurisprudence Say?[32]

Divorce under its different forms constitutes a classic example of the gap that exists between the principles established by the Qur'ān and the laws that have been elaborated by Muslim jurists in collections of Muslim law. Indeed, while the Qur'ān and the *hadīth* affirm, as we have seen, the equality of both partners in terms of divorce, *Fiqh* has reduced *talāq* to a restrictive juridical concept, namely repudiation, unilateral, and available only to the husband. In doing so, the Qur'ānic prescriptions that advanced women's rights have been reduced to specified discretionary and secondary formulations and in some cases were simply ignored under the pressure of local customs (*'urf*). The patriarchal power has thus succeeded in maintaining the ancient, pre-Islamic legal norms, repudiation by the husband, by transforming the *talāq* as it was advocated in the Qur'ān into a unilateral divorce, established as the arbitrary right of the husband and subject to his absolute authority.

---

[32] This is not a matter of a thorough and exhaustive reading of numerous legal texts of *Fiqh*, which would require a full study. The intention here is just to demonstrate how, generally speaking, the legal interpretations of the scriptural text of Islam have strayed from the original Qur'ānic vision.

In the vast majority of *Fiqh* books, *talāq* is defined as primarily a right exercised by the man, while a woman's right to divorce is described as "exceptional." This rule, which is found in almost all legal interpretations, cites two primary reasons on the basis of which it claims that the debate is closed and from there determines the direction of all laws relating to divorce in favor of the man.

The first reason, mentioned in all *Fiqh* books, is the innate weakness of a woman, described as "a being without a will, with very unstable moods, indecisive, impulsive, and whatever her degree of wisdom might be, remains impressionable and therefore unable confidently to manage marital conflict." According to this vision, "the woman does not possess qualities of resistance and endurance, which are reserved for the man, and this is why God has not given her the right to decide her fate, because given her weaknesses and flaws, she cannot use it wisely."[33]

The second reason that justifies why men were granted the exclusive right of divorce relates, according to legal interpretations, to the authority of the husband in the marital home. Keeping with the same vision, God has designed men as the "ultimate provider within the family, the one who has the ability and the power to maintain the home and to be responsible for his wife and the entire family." Thereby, it appeared logical, given all of his responsibilities, that the husband be the sole holder of the power to repudiate because "he will be wiser and will show more restraint in his decision making," while the wife, "being free of all responsibilities and given her excessive emotionality, is not in a position to demonstrate either lucidity, or wisdom before such ordeals."[34]

This type of rationalization regarding the incapacity of women to control their sentiments and to make rational decisions is the very foundation of a universal patriarchal culture, a culture that has guarded the mistaken notion that it would be in the interest of women to deny them the right to divorce, to protect them from themselves, and to spare them the adverse consequences they would suffer by using this right thoughtlessly. This in turn justifies keeping divorce in the hands of men, who are better at controlling their sentiments and deciding the future of their family.

---

[33] Cf. Abd ar-Rahmān al-Jazīrī, op. cit., p. 205, and Abd al-Karīm Hāmidī, *Maqāsid al-qurʾān min tashrīʾ al-Ahkām* (Dar Ibn Hazm, 2008), p. 350.

[34] Ibid.

It should be noted, however, that the Islamic law could not completely ignore the principles of the Qur'ān and the *hadīth*, which put an end to the blatant discrimination against women that was very prevalent in pre-Islamic Arabia and introduced a completely new conception of the role of women and men, within the family and in society, as a whole.

Traditional *Fiqh* was established taking into account the habits and customs of the tribal Arab society, which, of course, it could neither avoid nor ignore. It was also influenced, to a certain degree, by the facts and figures brought about by the new revelation. Thus, while the legal doctrine of *Fiqh* concerning divorce, which was detailed, complex, and prolific, continued to award men privileges that were denied to women, it managed to open new outlets to women and even grant them some rights, although minor. The most prominent example is allowing women to stipulate the inclusion of a clause in their marriage contracts that would give them the right to divorce, a type of divorce that is referred to as *tamlīq*. Such a condition in the marriage contract would allow women to terminate their conjugal union for justified causes such as the lack of proper maintenance, the absence of the husband, injury suffered by the wife, chronic illness, or a breach to one of the conditions stipulated in the marriage contract. Thus, while the vast majority of interpretations were discriminatory and far removed from the founding principles of the spiritual message of Islam, certain provisions of the Islamic law managed to be quite pioneering, compared to pre-Islamic patriarchal traditions.

Understandably, given the context, classic jurists did not elaborate upon this type of interpretation, more or less too liberal for the period, and might not have accepted it had it not been permitted by the Qur'ān and the *hadīth*. Nevertheless, despite this allowance, Muslim law could not totally liberate itself from the hostile context of the emancipation of women. So, while it might have resigned itself to this new egalitarian vision, it continued to privilege the customary law. Either way, the legal provisions that were crafted specially for women were always difficult to concretize when faced with on-the-ground realities.

To start a life together, under a marriage contract that stipulates a series of conditions, such as the unilateral right to divorce, among others, is not exactly complete or considered in good form for the vast majority of Muslim women. Furthermore, it is not that easy to prove the "shortcomings" of the conjugal duties of a husband; examples of divorce appeal from women that remain in suspense for years abound in Muslim countries where women struggle to make their voices heard while the men can get their divorce in a quarter of that time.

These social inequities are created by the legal complications of a *Fiqh* that has obstructed individual liberties, especially those of women, and nourished the idea that while divorce is a right of men, women are allowed such rights only exceptionally, to the detriment of their most basic rights. And how can one accept this type of archaic jurisprudence when the sources and the references that are supposedly behind these very laws of divorce, namely the Qur'ān and the *hadīth*, grant women standards that are not only egalitarian but also of eloquent simplicity? And how can we accept these legal provisions that are "crafted" for women while the Qur'ān, as we have seen, has given them exactly the same rights as men, in matters of divorce?

It is therefore imperative for us to go back to the spirit of the Sacred text that offers every leeway in terms of equal rights of men and women within marriage. Islamic law interpretation should therefore be reformed accordingly and freed from antiquated interpretations so that it is able to accompany contemporary challenges and be consistent with the purposes of the Qur'ānic message.

CHAPTER 11

The Shared Responsibility of Men and Women

It is distressing that certain verses in the Qur'ān that are very clear in terms of their encouragement of equality between men and women have been rather marginalized, infrequently cited, and even undervalued, at times, in Islamic thought. This is the case of a verse unequivocally considered the standard that lays the common ground for equality between men and women:

> But the believing men and believing women, are protectors of one another, enjoining right and forbidding wrong, performing the prayer, giving the alms, and obeying God and His messenger. They are those upon whom God will have mercy. Truly God is Mighty, Wise.[1]

The term *awliyā'* which, in this verse, signifies the covenant—mutual assistance and reinforcement—is derived from the Arabic root *w-l-y* and is the plural of the term *waliyy*, which is one of the names of God: *al-waliyy*, He who reinforces, protects, and supports.

More commonly, the word *waliyy* designates he who manages, he who has the aptitude to represent a minor, the guardian, he who has the capacity to administer or to govern, and he who can be entrusted, among others, with affairs of the state. Other derivatives of this term may also be cited such as *walā'*, which equally means closeness, friendship, loyalty, and trustworthiness; in its legal formulation, the term *wilāya*

---

[1] The Qur'ān 9:71.

© The Author(s) 2018
A. Lamrabet, *Women and Men in the Qur'ān*,
https://doi.org/10.1007/978-3-319-78741-1_11

designates the highest level of political governance (Muslim jurists speak of *wilāya 'amma*, "general or public governance"). In this register, one finds several types of *wilāya*: the Caliph, the Judge (*Qādi*), and the Administrator of Finances (*muhtasib*).

It is important to note that this verse was not revealed for a particular occasion or purpose. It was pronounced in order to change attitudes and states of mind so that a new vision of the relations between men and women may take root in the minds of the faithful by introducing this divine principle—the equality of sociopolitical participation. The verse starts with a major prescription that invites men and women to be and remain mutually supportive of one another, by virtue of a spiritual alliance or perhaps even complicity between them, based on a shared faith in God and His Prophet. The verse speaks of men and women believers whose hearts are united through sentiments of love, affection, and esteem, and this link between them is made easier by their faith.[2] It is a "proximity of kindness" that is suggested by the term *awliyā'*, "protectors of one another," where one perceives this subliminal proximity between men and women, in fellowship and harmony.

In this verse, the *wilāya* embodies the powerful alliance and proximity of the hearts of men and women, as willed by the Creator—a proximity of hearts that facilitates the shared management of daily affairs but also, as stated at the end of the verse, the management of the collective expression of faith through acts of worship such as prayer, almsgiving, and deep piety. This *wilāya*, which brings together hearts and actions, is nothing but the effective commitment to equality between men and women, an equality that is translated into one's everyday life via concrete actions of human solidarity; in such milieu, the only relevant criteria are hard work, honesty, and moral integrity.

It is important to note that while (or because) the gender equality significance of this verse (9:71), especially in the management of the sociopolitical public space, is clear, even indisputable, it has been mostly overlooked or ignored in the classic exegesis or *tafsīr*. And when it is included, it tends to be interpreted rather vaguely.

It is true that, generally speaking, classic exegesis or *tafsīr* has recognized that a degree of spiritual equality between men and women is a foundation of Islam. Here, they are essentially speaking in reference to

---

[2] Cf. *Tafsīr ash-Shawkānī*, commentary on verse 71 of *sūrah* 9.

religious practice and in terms of reward and punishment in the hereafter. However, it is the only manner of equality between men and women that has been recognized by most commentators because it was for them a matter of finding a religious compromise between cultural equality and the traditional hierarchical complementarity, which in most cases was and remains to be the norm. This hierarchical complementarity was always understood as a reflection of the traditional division of roles and responsibilities between couples but also in public life where the women were always confined to "secondary" positions, in comparison with the roles that are considered as priorities and hence ascribed to men.

Essentially, Islamic thinking was and remains marked by this unequal distinction between men and women. This makes it rather difficult to discuss or even imagine true gender equality, outside of what is known as "spiritual" equality. According to this vision, women cannot aspire to be or become anything but subordinates to men, who embody the norm and are thus the rightful possessors of responsibility and power on earth. And this is why most *tafāsīr* (commentaries) have interpreted this verse as referring, more or less, to spiritual equality, especially in relation to worship (*ʿibādāt*), to the extent that the verse mentions the ritual prayer (*salāt*) and the purification tax (*zakāt*). According to this outlook, men and women stand together (united, equal) only in the performance of acts of worship, especially through religious practices such as the *salāt* and *zakāt*.

Now, this verse affirms a prescription of vital importance, a prescription that precedes the mention of religious acts and rites, thereby asserting it as an independent concept: "But the believing men and believing women, are protectors of one another, enjoining right and forbidding wrong." The Qur'ān thus describes in equal terms the ideal men and women believers as, above all, persons who provide mutual support to each other, partake in the Common Good, and do not commit evil deeds. It is only after outlining this does the verse mention the performance of religious rites, in unity and solidarity.

Ibn Kathīr is among the few commentators who draw attention to two important elements in this verse. First, he reminds us that what has been evoked here is identical to what the Prophet described in one of his famous *hadīths* in which he confirms: "Believers in their mutual love, support, mercy and compassion are like the human body: when one organ suffers, the rest of the body develops a fever."[3] Even standing alone, this *ḥadīth*, through the metaphor of the human body, sums up an important aspect of human relationships: be aware of one another at all times. Via this *ḥadīth*, the Prophet of Islam wanted to educate men and women believers about this invaluable human value that makes people empathize and without which it would be difficult to talk about "spiritual cohabitation."

Ibn Kathīr's second remark is related to the command encouraging the Common Good: "Let there be among you a community calling to the good [*al-ma'rūf*], enjoining right, and forbidding wrong [*al-munkar*]. It is they who shall prosper."[4] Most Muslim scholars say that the verse deals with one of the most important Qur'ānic principles, as it aims at the establishment of justice and general welfare (*al-maslaha*) within the society or community in which one lives, which is one of the fundamental aims and principles of Islam. Here, it should be recalled that the order urging believers to encourage and practice the Common Good is something that is addressed frequently in the Qur'ān; hence, the recommendation has been treated and interpreted at length by most commentators.[5]

It is interesting to see how this Qur'ānic principle of encouraging the Common Good and advising against harmful practices (*al-amr bl-il-ma'rūf wa anahy 'ani-l-munkar*)—which is, strictly speaking, identical to the message expressed in the verse concerning the *wilāya* between male and female believers—has been widely pondered, analyzed, commented on, and recorded in the various exegeses (*tafāsīr*). In fact, this Qur'ānic injunction is considered by most commentators to be of paramount importance because it is through its concrete application, on the ground of social realities, that one would be able to measure the degree of the commitment of individuals to the edification of a just and morally equitable society.

All of the exegeses agree that this concept encompasses all of the ethical values related to human relationships, which is in fact a true pillar of Islam. A large number of *ḥadīths* also insist on this responsibility. The Prophet is reported to having repeated that a people who lose this

---

[3] An authentic *ḥadīth*, cited in the commentary of Ibn Kathīr on verse 71 of *sūrah* 9.

[4] The Qur'ān 3:104.

[5] Cf. particularly the Qur'ān 3:110, 114.

"mindfulness" of a commitment in favor of the Common Good and against harmful actions are a people "lost," in the sense that one loses the necessary qualities for the realization of a noble community life, ethically speaking.[6]

When someone asked the Prophet who was the best Muslim, the Prophet responded: "It is he who promotes the Common Good and advises again harmful actions."[7] And 'Alī[8] (Prophet Muhammad's cousin and son-in-law) is reported to having said: "The best of *jihād* is inciting the Common Good and refusing (to do) harmful actions."[9]

Al-Hussein (the son of 'Alī and Fātima and the grandson of the Prophet) considered this principle to be an integral part of priorities in the life of a Muslim, because it is from this "active consciousness" of individuals toward their collectivity that the fundamental equilibrium of a just society is erected. He also affirmed that this Qur'ānic principle allows the equitable distribution of wealth and enables one to avoid the mischief of oppression and political injustice.[10]

According to the nearly unanimous view of commentators, this duty is part of the overall framework of political and social action that urges Muslims to foster ethical values and respect for others, to be open to the world, to always seek knowledge, to act for the Common Good, and to denounce injustice wherever it comes from, and never to remain silent in the face of oppression and social or political discrimination and injustice.

So, even though most commentators agree about the importance of this Qur'ānic principle in the life of every Muslim, they differ about who

---

[6] *Tafsīr Ibn Kathīr*, commentary on verse 104 of *sūrah* 3.

[7] A *hadīth* cited by Zamakhsharī in his *Tafsīr*.

[8] 'Ali ibn Abī Tālib (60–661), reported to having been the first young male to accept Islam, was the cousin and son-in-law of Muhammad and the fourth of the rightly guided caliphs (*Rāshidūn*), a title reserved to the first four successors of the Prophet. In the midst of the civil unrest of 661, 'Ali was assassinated while praying in the Great Mosque of Kufa, Iraq, and died a couple of days later. While important to Sunni Muslims as the fourth and last rightly guided caliph, Shi'ites regard him as the first *Imām* after Muhammad. This disagreement caused a major split of the Muslim community into the Sunni and Shī'ite branches.

[9] Cited by Zamakhsharī. The term *jihād* mentioned here has to be understood in its etymological sense, that is the intellectual effort exerted by the faithful to understand and reflect on the meaning of life, to fight against one's own negative impulses, and to act positively within a society.

[10] At-Tabarsī, *majma' al-bayān fī tafsīr al-Qur'ān*, 1:483.

has the responsibility to implement such a principle. In other words, should the responsibility fall solely on a politically engaged erudite elite, or should it be generalized to all Muslims, regardless of their sociocultural status? Some affirm that the entire Muslim community is concerned while others insist that the responsibility lies with a particular group of people who have the obligation to take the initiative and to orient and guide the rest of the community.[11] Many other Muslim scholars assert that anyone endowed with reason and meet the requirements of honesty, intellectual integrity, and discernment, that is, any morally responsible person, must comply with this order.

Ibn 'Ashūr specifies that this Qur'ānic injunction is a binding obligation to all members of the community, each according to his capacities and potentials and with each person bringing in his "building block," in line with his particular areas of competence.[12] We thus see in most classic commentaries that the divine order to serve the Common Good and refrain from harmful actions, reiterated repeatedly in the Qur'ān, whether understood as an obligation of sociopolitical action that the entire community should tackle or a responsibility that is limited to a much smaller elite group, would be the assurance of minimal conditions of social justice and prosperity in a given society.

It is, however, astonishing to note that this same exhortation in the verse that speaks of the alliance between men and women, male and female believers, does not result in the same degree of commentary, with the exception of Ibn Kathīr who carefully references other interpretations.

Thus, the same expression reiterated by the Qur'ān is understood differently as soon as it deals with a prescription that calls on men and women in an egalitarian manner. In other words, when the Qur'ān exhorts believers in general to implement this principle, as done in verse 104 of *sūrah* 3, such prescription is interpreted as if it is destined uniquely to men, even though, in the opinion of the same assembly of Muslim scholars, the Qur'ān mostly calls on men and women under the general designation of "believers" (*al-mu'minūn*), and that such calling involves women in the same way and to the same degree as men.[13]

[11] Among those of this point of view is Tabarī and Ibn 'Atiyya.

[12] Ibn 'Ashūr, *At-tahrīr was at-tanwīr*, commentary on the verse.

[13] All of the words of God contained in the Qur'ān are addressed in exactly the same way, to men and to women: "When God says: 'O you the people!' or 'O you believers!' without

It must be stated that, even though the Qur'ān clearly calls men and women to encourage them, together, to work for the Common Good and refrain from harmful actions, the interpretation made by the assembly of classic commentators departs from that logic to the point that this requirement is confined to the field of religious practices and worship.

Now, without the smallest doubt, this verse very clearly addresses the shared commitment of men and women in sociopolitical action before it proceeds to speak about religious practices. Moreover, certain contemporary commentaries (*tafāsīr*) return to the first meaning of the verse and confirm that this Qur'ānic order for sociopolitical participation joins men and women. The Egyptian reformist Rachīd Ridā comments on the verse, saying: "This verse prescribes to women and men the responsibility of commanding the good and forbidding evil deeds, by means of words, writings, but also criticism addressed to political leaders, caliphs, kings, princes, or others. Women during the period of Revelation were very aware of this duty, and they put it into practice."[14] And Sheikh Ahmad Kuftaro[15] addresses the same question: "God has knowingly mentioned women in this verse, to insist on their effective participation in so far as the term *mu'minīn*, 'believers' naturally encompasses women."[16]

In his interpretation of the same verse, Hussein Fadlallah talks about a "coalition" between women and men in their belief (*wilāyat īmān*). He explains that men and women, united via intellectual, spiritual, and social ties, will attempt to improve their society. "Women and men have the mutual responsibility of being active in their society, in order to establish justice and to struggle against all tyrannies." He goes on to specify that "this verse reaffirms the egalitarian vision of the Qur'ān that incites women to get involved in all areas of their social and political life, contrary to the traditional exclusivist vision which tended to reduce women to their roles of mothers and wives; while they are of great importance, these functions cannot be their sole outlook."[17] By the means of a

---

a doubt, women are involved," explains Yūsuf al-Qaradhāwi in *Min fiqh ad-dawla fī-l Islām* (Dār ash-shurūq, 1998), p. 171.

[14] Abou Chouqqa, *Encyclopédie de la femme en islam*, vol. 2 (1998), p. 646.

[15] A Naqshbandi Sufi, Ahmed Kuftaro (1915–2004) was the Grand Mufti of Syria, the Head of the Supreme Council of Fatwa.

[16] See the interpretation of the entire verse on Kuftaro's site: www.kuftaro.org.

[17] www.arabic.bayyanat.org.lb/books/quran/altawba25.htm.

contextual reading, we can compare the concept of *wilāya* to the notion of equal citizenship as conceived in modern democratic systems.

As we conclude this analysis of the different interpretations, this verse is essential in its formulation of the equality between men and women, especially in the sociopolitical space. The Qur'ānic injunction cannot be clearer, as it inaugurates a new conception of male–female relations, including the fact that they enjoy equal rights to participate in political decision making. This concept is totally revolutionary and pioneering, even in terms of our modern times where equality of rights in terms of political participation at a global scale is not a given and appears to be the main obstacle to women's rights in most societies.[18]

The Qur'ān's call for the co-responsibility of men and women in the political management of their societies is the equivalent of the key principle of democratic requirement—the equal responsibility of all citizens. It is in this sense that the Qur'ānic concept of *wilāya* can be understood in our Muslim societies of today, in pursuit of democracy as the corollary of egalitarian citizenship.

When the Qur'ān entreats men and women believers to "Let there be among you a community calling to the good [*al-ma'rūf*], enjoining right, and forbidding wrong [*al-munkar*]. It is they who shall prosper," it is the active sociopolitical participation that is being addressed. Men and women, according to the vision of the Qur'ān, must equally participate in the management of political affairs and in political decision making. This citizenry involvement allows members of a community to move the society closer to the realization of the ideal of the Common Good while, at the same time, struggling against all of the obstacles that inhibit its evolution; unfortunately, in most Muslim countries, this noble societal notion of the Qur'ān has been scarified through the appalling political management of these societies that have instead been undermined by political dictatorship regimes. And this is precisely where the tragic political history in the land of Islam resides and where this Qur'ānic order has hardly ever been implemented, perhaps with the exception of the reign of the first rightly guided caliphs (*Rāshidūn*).

---

[18]The example of France is quite revealing: "Gender balance in politics is 10 years old. The representation of women is progressing, but slowly. We still have only 18.5% of women in the Assembly and 21.8% in the Senate. ... Parity remains a difficult goal to achieve." https://www.inegalites.fr/.

It is evident that this Qur'ānic injunction that encourages the equal participation of men and women in political affairs has never been to the taste of despotic regimes. Moreover, the scope of the concept of *wilāya*, in its promotion of sociopolitical participation sense, has been exceedingly reduced throughout the course of the history of Islamic civilization, dropping from its universal, political, and intellectual dimension to the limited domain of religious practice (*al-wilāya ad-dīniyya*).[19]

The rational interpretation of this verse, like so many others related to justice and equality, could not go beyond the intricacies of the political powers where these principles have gone astray, reduced to a single order: fear and absolute obedience due to the government, regardless of the injustice and exploitation that leaders might inflict upon their peoples. The great majority of Muslims are unaware that they have a say, granted by Islam, in the management of the political affairs that affect them, because they are educated to understand and experience[20] religion only under the register of fear and blind obedience.

The concept of the *wilāya* is used in this verse in its broadest sense, encompassing all actions that permit the positive evolution of a society at a given moment of history. It is, at once, political citizenship and daily citizenship. The most important point here is that women and men are challenged as equals to be the principal agents of change in their society. The concept of *wilāya* as used in this verse indicates the necessity of perfectly equal political partnership between men and women in the management of the sociopolitical space in which they operate. But, as with other principles stated in the Qur'ān, it is distressing to see that this verse, despite all that it carries in terms of egalitarian concepts such as political partnership, citizenship, and political action in favor of the Common Good, has not been valorized in Islamic thinking.

In short, this concept has hardly ever been accorded the importance it merits, compared to other secondary principles that, with the passage of time, have become priorities in the minds of a large number of

---

[19] The Moroccan historian Abdallah Laroui addresses this issue in his book *As-sunna wal-islāh* (Al-markaz ath-thaqāfī al-'arabī, 2008), p. 158.

[20] See the pertinent analysis of Fatima Mernissi in *Islam et démocratie*, Albin Michel, Espaces libres, Paris, where she affirms: "Islam is probably the only monotheist religion where scientific exploration is systematically discouraged, if not banned, because a rationally analyzed Islam would be difficult to put in the service of despots. ... It is the fear of the *Imām*."

Muslims by the force of a literalist ideological propaganda, the fruit of a deplorable intellectual impoverishment of Islamic thought.[21]

In fact, for a very long time now, the holistic meaning of this concept has been downplayed by most of the erudite Muslims, in favor of a much narrower interpretation that confines the equality between men and men in the Qur'ān to the field of worship. Hence, it is essential, at present, to reread this verse and to restate the principles it holds, especially since they are extraordinarily timely and particularly significant in the contemporary Muslim context. It is also urgent that this concept of *wilāya* reacquires its importance and, once again, becomes a central concept in male–female relations and interaction. It is by reference to this fundamental concept that all the other Qur'ānic concepts concerning women must be reread and redefined in order to rediscover and reestablish the egalitarian spirit that underlies the spiritual message of Islam. Moreover, it is through this principle that all other issues concerning women and men, many of which are inherent in the conjunctures of the time, can be analyzed and duly understood in the present context.

---

[21] This is especially the case of Qur'ānic concepts related to the ethics of the body (which concerns men as well as women), which have been reduced to the sole theme of the "*hijāb*" for women, even though this issue remains secondary in comparison with many other Qur'ānic principles, including that of the *wilāya*. We will come back to this theme later on.

CHAPTER 12

The Management of Public and Private Spheres

Beyond dispute, the concept of *qiwāma*, a husband's moral and financial responsibility to his family, occupies a prominent seat among the arguments that, while derived from the Qur'ān, are rehashed and then pushed forward by some *'ulamā* as well as by "ordinary mortals," as evidence of male power, to demonstrate, in "Islamic" terms, the "absolute superiority" of men to women. For centuries now, this has been one of the strongest preconceived notions that has molded the minds of many Muslims, men and women. According to this predisposition, the Qur'ān has definitively decreed the absolute authority of husbands over their wives, and for some, even the authority of **all** men over **all** women.

The notion of *qiwāma* is derived from the Qur'ānic term *qawwāmūn* or *qawwāmīn*, both of which are the plural forms of the term *qawwām*, constructed from the root *q-w-m*. As indicated earlier in this book, Arabic word roots can have up to thirty meanings, such as in this case, stand up, carry out, undertake, accomplish, perform, recover, rebel, provide, support, and bear. The term *qawwāmūn* or *qawwāmīn*—whose linguistic form expresses the perfection of the action that had been undertaken, expressed by the verb *qāma*—has appeared three times in the Qur'ān.

The most cited and best-known verse that has been used to affirm the supremacy of men over women uses the concept of *qiwāma* in the following manner: "Men are the upholders and maintainers [*qawwāmūn*] of women by virtue of that in which God has favored some of them above others [*ba'dahum 'alā ba'd*] and by virtue of their spending from their

© The Author(s) 2018
A. Lamrabet, *Women and Men in the Qur'ān*,
https://doi.org/10.1007/978-3-319-78741-1_12

wealth (for the support of women)."[1] There are two other verses in the Qur'ān that speak of the same concept, as follows:

> O you who believe! Be steadfast [*qawwāmīn*] maintainers of justice, witnesses for God, though it be against yourselves, or your parents and kinsfolk, and whether it be someone rich or poor, for God is nearer unto both. So follow not your caprice, that you may act justly. If you distort or turn away, truly God is Aware of whatsoever you do.[2]
>
> O you who believe! Be steadfast [*qawwāmūn*] for God, bearing witness to Justice, and let not hatred for a people lead you to be unjust. Be just; that is nearer to reverence. And reverence God. Surely God is Aware of whatsoever you do.[3]

QIWĀMA IN THE PUBLIC SPHERE

Before we carry out a close examination of the first of the three verses cited previously that are believed to uphold and support masculine authority and to remain faithful to the overall approach of the Qur'ān and its internal cohesion, we must start with a careful examination of the concept of *qiwāma*, as presented in the verse, in light of the two other verses that use the same term—*qiwāma*—but where there is a large consensus among the *'ulamā* that they address both men and women: "O you who believe!"

Concerning the two Qur'ānic verses (4:135 and 5:8), most commentators agree that they represent a divine call addressed to all believers, men and women, telling them to respect the primary values of justice, equality, and impartiality. In both verses, the initial injunction—*kūnū qawwāmīn*—is used. In the first verse, the phrase that is used is *kūnū qawwāmīna bi-l-qist*, which means "be strict and rigorous in the application of your sense of equality and justice." In the second verse, *kūnū qawwāmīna shuhadā'a lillāh* can be translated as "be determined and meticulous in your testimony."

In both verses, the unconditional respect for these values, equality and justice, is reiterated, relentlessly emphasizing their great importance, including when the testimony is given for oneself, regarding

---

[1] The Qur'ān 4:34.

[2] Ibid.:135.

[3] The Qur'ān 5:8.

relatives, or regarding others, whether rich or poor. The reliability of testimony should be upheld even if it might help an enemy or benefit people toward whom one may feel resentment or dislike, for one reason or another.

Furthermore, it would be useful to recall the circumstances of the revelation of verse 135 of *sūrah* 4, including time and place. According to the narration, two men, one rich and the other poor, came to the Prophet to settle a dispute. The prophet settled it in favor of the poor man, reasoning that, all things being equal, the poor man was not in a position to be unjust.[4]

The verse was revealed to incite believers, men and women, not to base their reasoning and decision making on values such as the wealth or poverty of the individual being judged; what should always preside is truthfulness and justice, not social relations and/or conditions. This principle is equally applicable to kinship affiliations, the prioritization and consideration of which often leads people to rule unfairly toward others: "though it be against yourselves or your parents and kinsfolk" declares the Qur'ān. In short, it is the spirit of equality that must always prevail, not family links and attachments. The strong emphasis that the Qur'ān places on the spirit of justice (*al-qist*) conveys the obligation to exercise moral uprightness, one that respects the equality and humanity of all human beings without exception.

It is reported that the second verse (5:8) was revealed at a time of a conflict between the Muslims and the Jewish tribe of Banī Nadhīr. The goal was to inspire Muslims to behave with integrity and good-will toward those who were in conflict with them at a given time. The Qur'ān urges them to remain fair and reasonable despite the feelings of resentment and animosity that existed between the two communities at that time.[5]

---

[4] See the *hadīth* reported by Asbāt in Tabarī, *jāmi' al-bayān fī ta'wīl al-qur'ān*, commentary on the verse.

[5] Ibid. According to another version, it was a polytheist tribe that opposed them the year of al-Hudaybiyyah. The Treaty of Hudaybiyyah (628) was the aftermath of the Prophet's and about 1400 followers' first attempt to perform the pilgrimage to Mecca. Having been humiliated the year before, after their failed attempt to besiege Medina, the Meccan leaders refused Muhammad entry into Mecca. Instead, a Meccan delegation met them about 9 miles outside of Mecca, at a site called al-Hudaybiyyah, where the Muslims had stopped. There, a 10-year treaty was concluded between the Prophet, representing the Muslim community in Medina, and the Meccan leaders. The Prophet agreed to forego the pilgrimage

So, the concept of *qiwāma* in these two verses is interpreted as the absolute demand for justice that should inspire the heart and conscience of all believers, men and women. This *qiwāma* or concern for fairness, justice, and the rigor of judgment is one of the major recommendations of the Qur'ānic message. This is where we see the profound sense of the term *qawwāmīn*, which suggests an impartial moral consciousness, in other words, self-perfection in relation to fairness and testimony.

The Qur'ān incites male and female believers to be the witnesses of truth and justice, even if such testimony goes against their personal desires and proper interests. The only thing that counts should be the total respect for this spirit of justice, which gives meaning to the expression of faith in one's heart and in one's acts. Justice and equity are thus the emblems of Islam. And the sum of this spiritual message is a reminder of the values that should constitute a principal dimension of the religious conscience of any man or woman of faith. These are the essential values of spirituality—*qiwāma* in justice, equity, and testimony, symbolizing the intrinsic value of the requirement that must animate the hearts and consciousness of men and women—the men and women that the Qur'ān urges to testify in the sense of justice at all times. Above all, spiritual commitment is to be an irreproachable and unchallengeable witness with one's self.

These are the values advocated by the Qur'ān in favor of a *qiwāma* of justice that must be part of the Islamic curriculum in the moral education of Muslims, men and women, who seem to have forgotten the fundamental principles of the Qur'ānic ethic in favor of clinging to religious practices that are sometimes drained of their soul. Muslims pray to God five times a day, respect the fast during the month of Ramadan, and memorize the Qur'ān, all of which are very important. However, this *qiwāma* of justice is virtually absent from their daily conduct.

One thus notes a huge gap between the religious practice and the sum of the Qur'ānic ethic, a gap that seems to deepen, day after day, throughout the entire Muslim world. This lag reduces the grandeur of this last monotheist revelation to a mere ritualized and formalized religious ceremony carried to excess. A *hadīth* of the Prophet affirms that an hour of

---

for that year on the condition that they be allowed to come back the following year, which they did.

justice is comparable to sixty years of religious practice.[6] While keeping in mind the undeniable importance of religious rites in the life of a practitioner, these rites are primarily the outward appearance of a spirituality that has value only if it results in moral conduct that is designed and performed in uprightness and self-sacrifice. Desperately seeking to master a rigorous religious practice without being aware of Qur'ānic values such as, among others, the *qiwāma* of justice and fairness is like severing the religion from much of its raison d'être.

This is the bitter truth that prompted contemporary scholars such as Malek Bennabi to write the following: "The Islamic ideal has sunk in the arrogance and self-sufficiency of the devout who believes that perfection is realized through the five daily prayers, without trying to amend or improve (his conduct). He is irrevocably perfect ... perfect as death or nothingness."[7]

Given this gloomy reality, it is important that future generations of Muslims, men and women, be reminded of all of these Islamic values so that they become fully aware of this consciousness of justice and fairness and apply it vis-à-vis all human beings, be they rich or poor, relatives or strangers, powerful or just one of the people, Muslims or non-Muslims. We must reconstruct the Muslim identity, torn between withdrawal and lethargy, based on these values that demand justice; educating Muslims to be righteous is the key to building moral societies. And it is precisely the deficit of this demand for justice, as portrayed in *qiwāma*, which today constitutes one of the greatest ordeals faced by Muslim societies, which are plagued by moral injustice on an alarming scale.

These two verses correspond to the vision of a much broader *qiwāma* concerning the public sphere (*al-qiwāma al-ʿāmma*), which women and men are expected to practice in their lives, on earth and in the hereafter, an extension of the fundamental spiritual dimension of the Qur'ānic ethic.

---

[6] An authentic *hadīth* reported by Abū Nuʿaym, *Fadīlat al-ʿādilīna min al-wulāt as-salatīn*, *hadīth* no. 12.

[7] Malek Bennabi, *Vocation de l'islam* (Albouraq, 2006), p. 126.

QIWĀMA IN THE PRIVATE SPHERE[8]

Having examined the meanings of the term *qawwāmīn* in the two preceding verses, we are now positioned to much better understand the first verse (4:34): "Men are the upholders and maintainers [*qawwāmūn*] of women by virtue of that in which God has favored some of them above others [*ba'dahum 'alā ba'd*] and by virtue of their spending from their wealth (for the support of women)."

The term *qawwāmīn*, in most French translations,[9] corresponds to the notions of "authority" or "command": "men have authority over women" or "men are responsible for the care and management of women." And it is in the sense of "authority" that virtually all of the interpretations of the verse, be they classic or contemporary, are directed.

In all of the interpretations that are covered by the classic exegeses, *qiwāma* in the sense of authority is conceived as a "privilege" granted to the husband and a divine favor accorded to him, the man, standing for all men. Most exegeses explain that this *qiwāma* is a function of the natural predisposition of a man to be the "chief" of the woman (*ra'īs*), her superior, he who leads and directs her (*al-ḥākim*), and he who has the right to "correct" her if she deviates from the right path.[10] Other commentators speak of the "control" or "hegemony" of men over the moral life of women.[11] According to this view, men have the right of "domination" over women in all spheres of social life.[12] Some commentators even go to the point of comparing a wife to a prisoner or a slave who should remain under the authority of a husband, who is described as the holder of absolute power.[13] And virtually all commentators agree that this is a privilege granted to men by God, beyond their roles as husbands. This preferential treatment of men, according to this outlook, is reinforced by the continuation of the same verse of the Qur'ān: *bi mā faddala Allāhu ba'dahum 'alā ba'd*, generally translated as follows: "Men are the upholders and maintainers [*qawwāmūn*] of women by virtue of that

---

[8] Several contemporary scholars have deconstructed the traditionalists' conception of *Qiwāma* by building it around these two dimensions, public (*'āmma*) and private (*Khāssa*).

[9] The same can be said of the English translations of the term.

[10] Cf. commentary of Ibn Kathīr of verse 34 of *sūrah* 4.

[11] Commentary of Ibn 'Abbās on the same verse.

[12] Commentary of Zamakhsharī.

[13] Ibn al-Qayyim al-Jawziya expresses it in such a way in *I'lām al-muwaqqi'īn*.

in which God has favored some of them above others [*ba'dahum 'alā ba'd*] and by virtue of their spending from their wealth (for the support of women)" (4:34). In sum, beyond any doubt, such verse confirms the supremacy of men over women.

In the same classic commentaries and according to most commentators, the preeminence of men is justified by a series of "aptitudes" that make them, by the force of circumstances and nature, superior to women. It is particularly interesting to examine some of the justifications that have been put forward and to recognize the state of mind that, through time, forged the dogmatic standards that justify, culturally and religiously, the superiority of men. For example:

- Men are naturally more gifted with reason than women. Among women, reason is rather deficient due to their excessive emotionality, and their tendency to resolve problems under the influence of their sentiments and not by reason.
- It is men who occupy positions of high political and judicial responsibility such as high commandery, governance, and the judiciary.
- Only men can claim the *Imāmate* in prayer, preaching the Friday sermon, or to function as a *muezzin* (calling Muslims to prayer from the *minarate* of a mosque).
- Prophecy is accorded only to men and never to women. Men go to war and have the right to booty. And the man's share of inheritance is twice that of a woman.
- Men give a dowry (*mahr*) to their wives. And men are gifted with a physical strength that is much superior to that of women.
- Men are always the guardians of women; the opposite is never possible.
- Polygamy is a man's right and a proof of his superiority. And "repudiation" is a man's unilateral right and privilege that is never extended to women.
- Men are much more naturally motivated to pursue learning, knowledge, and sciences than women. And the constitutional weakness of women is a natural attribute that results from their physical and biological constitution.[14]

---

[14] This type of affirmation appears in the classical works of commentaries on the Qur'ān, like those of Tabarī, Ibn Kathīr, and Qurtubi. In this regard, we will pass over some ridiculous statements such as "men are superior to women because they are the ones who grow a beard and wear a turban."

This list is an example of the reasons or evidence employed by commentators to argue and to demonstrate the natural eminence of men. For them, the *qiwāma* of men over women invoked in the verse was but a further confirmation of all of their suppositions. Thus, without contest, this verse became the reference that shaped all of their family-related interpretations. Furthermore, all other Qur'ānic verses that concerned women were read and understood from the perspective of *qiwāma* construed as the "right" of men over women.

In other words, this verse was interpreted as a commandment of God, granting man the right to be the absolute commander over women, thereby also conferring on him an absolute moral and material authority. And since men have the authority as custodians of their families, of which the wife is a member, in gratitude, she must categorically and merrily submit to his masculine authority. Such male authority is also manifest in the marriage contract that confirms the husband's absolute rights over the wife, who belongs to him, just as much as any other commodity he might have acquired, body and soul, as of the moment he assumes his financial obligations (*nafaqa*) toward her.

This rather abusive interpretation of this notion of *qiwāma* in the classic commentaries has legitimized the effective superiority of men, which in turn sanctioned the obedience (*tā'a*) obligation of the wife, as *tā'a* and *qiwāma* became corollaries of one another. This, in turn, has contributed to the blossoming of a religious literature that is derogatory toward women, with the end result being the obstruction of the social and legal implementation of the liberating spirit of the Qur'ānic message concerning the status of women within their families and their lives as couples.

Moreover, it became increasingly standard in certain religious writings to read assertions such as "the road to Paradise for a wife is through her obedience to her husband," a declaration that contradicts one of the principle tenets of Islam—obedience and submission are due to God and God only—and undermines the principle of the oneness of God (*tawhīd*), the foundation on which rests the entire spiritual dimension of Islam.

It is important to keep in mind here that the interpretation of this concept of *qiwāma*, with all of its negative insinuations concerning the social status of women, was construed and elaborated in the framework of a political reappropriation whose objective was completely removed from the emancipatory vocation, which was and remains to be a primary

Qur'ānic message. So, while the Revelation incited believers to liberate their slaves, certainly the women among them, and considered such liberation a profound act of piety, shortly thereafter, facilitated by the rapid expansion of the Muslim Empire, we start to witness an absolute regression, such as the procurement of female slaves (*jāriyāt*), rapidly becoming a symbol of the wealth and opulence of autocratic rulers.[15]

Thus, it was in response to new social norms typified by the presence of women slaves, cloistered in palaces, and the confiscation of political consultation (*shūra*)—another Qur'ānic principle—that the commentators and jurists would extend the significance of concepts such as *qiwāma*, which has become synonymous with *sulta*, or the unconditional "authority" of autocratic rulers in the public sphere and a corresponding one in the private sphere. In fact, under the influence of patriarchal social customs on the one hand and the existing governance system (*hākimiyya*) on the other, husbands were deliberately compared to the *hākim*, in other words, the head of state. In a new autocratic political system with despotic rulers, *qiwāma* came to represent such authority, and by extrapolation, it became associated with the same type of despotic authority exercised on the home front.

This dominant/submissive relationship, simultaneously exercised at the highest political levels and at the household level, ends up justifying and bolstering the existence of the other: Family-level despotism headed by an all-powerful husband and a submissive and obedient wife is fertile ground for the launch and standardization of autocratic political systems. Submission becomes the norm at both the household and state levels. Children who grow up within never-challenged familial despotism learn to accept and to consider as natural the despotism of the political elite. They are the two sides of the same coin; both are seen as emanating from the same holy order.

This forcibly brings us back to the meaning given to the term *qawamūn* in the verse, which has always been interpreted as signifying "authority." "Men are the upholders and maintainers [*qawwāmūn*] of women by virtue of that in which God has favored some of them above others [*ba'dahum 'alā ba'd*] and by virtue of their spending from their wealth (for the support of women)." According to the general context of this verse, *qawwāmūn* more exactly signifies "*provide*" or "support,"

---

[15] The Qur'ān encourages the liberation of slaves (see, e.g., 2:177; 90:13; 9:60).

an interpretation that is supported by the continuation of the verse that speaks about the expenditures that men make from what they own. Thus, the men provide for or support their extended families and wife and children.

Here, we are at the very heart of a Qur'ānic dimension that should be fully assimilated to better understand the principles whence generated. Indeed, this is in reference to the exemption granted to women with respect to the family financial weight. We see here how the Qur'ān is putting itself into the sociocultural context of the era, in Arabia and elsewhere at that time, when, in general, the financial responsibility of the family rested on the shoulders of the husband, considered the household head. This is the classic image of a social hierarchy that endures despite the major socioeconomic transformations occurring in the world.

We must also pay close attention to the expression that follows the term *qawwāmūn: bi mā faddala Allāhu ba'dahum 'alā ba'd*, which is often interpreted to mean: "by virtue of that in which God has favored some of them above others [*ba'dahum 'alā ba'd*]." The "favored" interpretation of the verse has been "because God has made some of them (men) surpass others (women)." However, the verse can also be interpreted as "because of the favors that God has accorded to certain men or women vis-à-vis other men or other women." The logic of the second interpretation lies in the fact that had the Qur'ān intended the reference to denote women as the "reigned" party, with men being the "leaders/controllers," which remains to be the dominant interpretation, it would have specified the femininity of the object by using the feminine pronoun "*-hinna*," "*ba'duhum 'alā ba'dihinna*." But the Qur'ān did not do that, and for very good reason: it never intended to single women out. This is the explanation given by the Muhammad 'Abduh, who affirms that this verse clearly suggests that "certain men were favored compared to some women and some women were favored compared to some men." So what we see is a mutual preference (of men and women), which corresponds much more with the equality spirit of the Qur'ān and with the reality of human societies.

Thus, when the verse is examined from within its proper context and reread in light of other verses, especially Qur'ānic concepts regarding marriage, which we have seen earlier, one starts to understand that, in fact, this *qiwāma* is not a privilege accorded by the Creator to men; it is rather an obligation in the sense that the husband is assigned the moral and material responsibility of satisfying the needs of his entire family, including his wife. So, contrary to the patriarchal interpretations of *qiwāma* that affirm the superiority of men to women, *qiwāma* denotes the responsibility of some, vis-à-vis others (*taklīf*), rather than an honor (*tashrīf*) bestowed on one party, vis-à-vis another.

In his commentaries on the Qur'ān, Sayyid Qutb examined the concept of *qiwāma* strictly within the framework of the institution of marriage, which reinforces the notion of a *qiwāma khāssa* (*private qiwāma*).[16] For Qutb, this verse should be read in light of the conjugal institution and affirms that the favor (*al-fadl*) accorded to the husband is due to his financial responsibility, while reminding one that the reward for such responsibility is not the wife's obedience but rather the respect of both partners for the conjugal commitment and for each other.[17]

Other contemporary commentators such as Mohammad Abduh and Muhammad Shaltūt have interpreted the concept of *fadl* (from the Arabic verb *faddala*, "to favor," which appears in the verse), as "additional" or "extra" (another meaning of the Arabic term *fadl*) responsibilities for the men. In other words, the *qiwāma* accorded to the husband is not because he is a man; rather, it is based on his ability to manage the financial resources of the household, for its [the household's] maintenance. This means that if the financial situation of the husband changes and he is no longer able to address the household's material needs (continue to serve the function of *qiwāma*), not an infrequent event in our modern societies, such responsibility will most likely fall on the shoulders of the wife, who then becomes the one exercising the function of *qiwāma*. In short, the *qiwāma* is not the exclusive right or responsibility of the man.[18]

Hence, in order to deconstruct the semantic confusion built around the *qiwāma* of men, we should start by limiting the use of the term to the private sphere of a conjugal household. Thus, the "material responsibility" exercised by the husband relates to the management of the household. And as this private *qiwāma* is exercised within the household unit,

---

[16] Sayyid Qutb, *Fī dhilāl al-qur'ān*, commentary on verse 34 of *sūrah* 4. Furthermore, other erudite contemporary commentators reinstate the *qiwāma* in the strict context of the conjugal/family life, as did Hussein Fadlallah, among others, in his interpretation of the verse.

[17] Ibid.

[18] Mahmound Hamdi Zakzouk, former Minister of Religious Affairs in Egypt, had said: "Every man does not necessarily cater to the needs of every women", www.icsfp.com.

whether extended or nuclear, it does not and should not, in the least, concern the sociopolitical public sphere that, as we have seen, must be managed by both women and men in accordance with the criteria of equality and justice. Thereafter, the private *qiwāma* should be analyzed and interpreted within the normative framework governing conjugal relationships, as we have already described under the Qur'ānic ethic of marriage.

It is in fact impossible to reach an impartial interpretation of the verse that speaks of *qiwāma* without taking into account its integrality and without considering the totality of the verses dealing with women, which stipulate equality and establish a true autonomy for women, unthinkable for the time period, whether in Arabia or elsewhere. Importantly, *qiwāma* should also be read in reference to Qur'ānic marriage ethics, in parallel with the notions of the "Common Good," and decorum, which comes back to the various Qur'ānic injunctions, directed to men, such as the verses that deal with life as a couple, divorce, nursing (a baby), or social cohabitation. All of these injunctions to men shared the common objective of a radical change of men's behavior toward women, and to introduce the Qur'ānic ethic principle of *ma'rūf* as a foundation for the relationship between men and women. Here, we need to remind ourselves that the word *ma'rūf* is mentioned more than twenty times in the Qur'ān, as opposed to the word *qiwāma*, which has not been mentioned but once, in that particular sense of the word, but which, as strange as this may seem, has taken, in its literal interpretation, a chauvinist and blown out of proportion importance in the Arab-Muslim mindset, in comparison with *ma'rūf*, which does not appear to have had a lasting impression.

We also need to know how to reread private *qiwāma* in parallel with other verses that deal with family life, such as those that incite husbands and wives to share responsibilities and practice mutual aid (*ba'duhum awliyā' ba'd*), love and tenderness (*rahma wa mawadda*), and especially mutual commitment and reciprocal consultation (*tashāwur wa tarādhī*). In this fashion, one would not be able to read the verse on *qiwāma*, which is interpreted classically as male authority, without also having considered, beforehand, another primary obligation decreed by the Qur'ān, that of justice (*al-'adl*), advocated throughout the revealed text as an indispensable prerequisite for all human relations.

Once the concept of *qiwāma* is reinstated in the framework of marriage, in accordance with the Qur'ānic principles, how could one accept or believe an argument that legitimizes the absolute authority of the husband, the blind submission of the wife, and masculine hegemony in marriage? And how would one accept justifications that invoke the natural weakness and inferiority of women, or to admit theories that are still in fashion in the current Islamic discourse, which see in every woman a creature stripped of reason, whose only calling is to "satisfy" a husband who is privileged, just because he is a man?

One cannot but wonder how such discriminatory allegations can be advanced, faced with the requirement for justice in the Qur'ān, the obligation of conjugal consultations, the principles of mutual responsibility, and the values of reciprocal love, of generosity, and of shared selflessness.

Qiwāma is thus not the assumed authority, granted to the husband, but the responsibility of maintaining the conjugal household, renowned since time immemorial, and representative, in all cultures, of a family environment. A social framework whereby the man, as a husband, father, or any other role, has the responsibility, not to mention the obligation and the duty, to meet the needs of his family—in short, to all kinfolks who are in need. This implication of the man in the management of the conjugal household is a way of balancing certain tasks in married life, which allows wives, certainly those who are of childbearing age, to focus on rearing the children, without any constraints.

However, the fact remains that, despite all the advances and achievements that allowed women to gain a certain financial and professional independence, the problem of sharing household responsibilities is far from settled. Professional parity has not resulted in domestic parity, contrary to the expectations or at least the hopes and aspirations of sociologists and feminists. Most working women are still unable to reconcile their professional life with their family life: It is the classic image of the double or even triple shift, trying to balance work and family, including rearing children. A study that was published by the review of *la Caisse nationale d'allocation familiale* (CAF; the National Fund of Family Benefits) in France summarizes the current reality in France thusly:

> The unequal distribution of parental work is unquestionable and, despite the discourse on equality and diversity, tasks remain very specialized: mothers take care of the daily tasks and (handle) the constraints associated with house work, while fathers invest in recreational activities.[19]

[19] *Le Monde*, April 8, 2009.

It is appropriate here to clarify that there are no verses in the Qur'ān that deal with the distribution of household tasks or assign specific functions to one or the other of the couple, nor to suggest that domestic work is the inalienable responsibility of women, as many Muslims believe. There is not even one verse that goes in that direction.

When Aïsha, the Prophet's wife, was asked about what the Prophet did, once he was at home, she responded: "he does the simple daily chores, such as washing his things, milking the sheep, mending his clothes, and serving his people (*kāna fī khidmati ahlihi*)."[20] Such was the behavior of one who applied the *qiwāma* within his family, despite being the messenger of the Creator. The *qiwāma* of the Prophet consisted of being at the service of his family. His was a *qiwāma* that was neither authoritarian nor despotic. He applied the spiritual message of Islam, including equality, in his everyday life. He understood that equality of all before God, of necessity, implied equality among all his creatures, men and women—equality every day, equality throughout life.

Via the notion of *qiwāma*, the Qur'ān insisted on the financial responsibility of men in the framework of conjugal life, especially during periods when women are physically vulnerable and require assistance, physically and morally, such as during pregnancy, childbirth, and nursing. It was also a way of acknowledging their efforts and compensating them for their work. Besides, it is also very much within the spirit of the Qur'ān to ensure the protection of the vulnerable, women, children, the elderly, anyone who should ever be in need, irrespective of the social conditions.

Hence, the financial responsibility is primarily the husband's to fulfill, irrespective of the wife's social or economic status. What wealth she might have should be protected by the husband but remain in her possession. Here, we see a general rule that grants women the primary right to protect themselves against any misfortune. Whatever the wife's revenues or profession might be, they have the advantage of always being able to benefit from familial financial support. This brings to mind some current feminists' insistence that women should be entitled to de facto equal treatment in all spheres of social life because, as women, they require additional provisions for maternity and reproductive health. This additional provision lies precisely in the *qiwāma*, which ensures, during

---

[20] *Hadīth* reported by Ahmad, at-Tirmidhī, and al-Bukhārī.

married life, moral and material security for the wife because of her specific responsibilities but which, unfortunately, was interpreted incorrectly in the sense of the authority of the husband. The financial responsibility was understood through a patriarchal prism as a privilege that was accorded to men.

Having said that, we should also be able to recognize that, like other Qur'ānic concepts, the interpretation and concrete expression of *qiwāma* evolved over time, especially since specific social roles have not been established and assigned by the Qur'ān. This concept should thus be reinterpreted in view of the practical necessities of our modern lives where both husband and wife are confronted by the daily reality in which the financial co-responsibility imposes itself by the force of circumstances.

So, should the private *qiwāma* within the family continue to be the unique responsibility of the husband, given prevailing conditions of, for example, job insecurity and such other financial hazards? It should surely be understood, nowadays, within the framework of the general responsibility, shared by the couple, of which the Qur'ān speaks in its marriage ethic. The *qiwāma* should be understood and interpreted as a *qiwāma* of mutual support and shared responsibility. Thus, it will become much more operational in our societies where the middle class is expanding and where both husband and wife join efforts to be able to assume, together, the economic burden of the family and the daily management of the household.[21]

Today, it is up to Muslims, men and women, to put the spirit of equality and justice, which underlies the Qur'ānic concept of *qiwāma*, back into practice in the framework of the modern conjugal life. For this to occur, just going back to the source—flushing out the different discriminatory interpretations that have distorted the meaning of *qiwāma*— will not suffice. We should also learn how to take into account new problems imposed by the globalization of our societies, whose negative

[21] This was how, in 2004, the new family code in Morocco replaced the old notion of the husband as "head of household" with co-responsibility, thus placing the family under the joint responsibility of both partners. It took fourteen centuries to comprehend that it was completely possible to find in the Qur'ān universal principles such as the equality of family responsibility. Let us recall that, in all other Muslim countries, the notion of the husband as head of household remains the case in the family code and is still regarded as an inalienable Islamic principle.

repercussions on the moral and economic stability of couples and families are becoming increasingly felt.

To conclude, it is evident that we cannot continue to reduce the multifaceted concept of *qiwāma* to the authority of the husband; as we have seen, such a reductionist and misleading interpretation amounts in fact to the violation of the spiritual principles of the Qur'ānic message concerning the ethic of the conjugal union. In the Qur'ān, *qiwāma* is a primary principle of the equality of men and women, including men's obligation to provide for the material needs of the entire household as a means of addressing the delicacy of the balance of power inherent in any marital relationship. This is the same ideal of equality, constantly renewed, to which the Qur'ān implores us to implement at any time and in any place.

CHAPTER 13

The Basic Verses on Inheritance

Women's share of the inheritance is half of men's. This is certainly among the best-known prescriptions of Islam and within which the entire question of Islamic inheritance has been defined. Let us state from the outset that the very complex inheritance law in Islam cannot be reduced to this simple formula that, while rather common, applies only to a specific type of cases. It is true that this division—with the man receiving twice the woman's share—appears unfair and should be reassessed, but within its appropriate context: the new inheritance law that was brought about by the Qur'ānic Revelation, which, for the very first time in the history of monotheism, gave women the right to inherit. From such a perspective, the entire body of the newly introduced inheritance law appears to be and should be considered revolutionary, having, in one stroke, dramatically improved the social status of women during this period of human civilization. Thus, to be able adequately to understand the objective of this Qur'ānic prescription, we must address it in its own spatiotemporal framework: seventh-century Arabia.

In fact, in the tribal society of the era, during which wars and looting were rampant and the most powerful in a society were the masters of all, women were among the most vulnerable, considered part and parcel of the captured spoils for winners and a potential source of shame and dishonor for losers. So, for families and kinfolk, women were considered a burden and, as such, were not endowed with any rights, let alone inheritance rights, as they, themselves, were part of some other person's inheritance—a man's. Yes, women were indeed a part of the "goods"

© The Author(s) 2018
A. Lamrabet, *Women and Men in the Qur'ān*,
https://doi.org/10.1007/978-3-319-78741-1_13

that men inherited at the death of the women's husbands. It is important to mention here that women were not the only members of the society who were excluded from the inheritance system; they were also joined by children, the elderly, and any other person who did not mount, carry a sword, or fight a battle. Only those who participated in the defense of the tribe had any inheritance rights.

Needless to say, this state of affairs was not specific to the Arabian Peninsula. In fact, it was the norm in the civilizations of that era—plunder economies in which physical force was master. This is the context within which we need to assess and reassess the contributions of the Qur'ān to this matter. It is also in this sense that we need to situate the issue of inheritance, keeping in mind that the Islamic Revelation, from the start, awarded women the right to inherit, a right that had never before been mentioned by any revealed text, ideology, or political system, and even less practiced. By granting women inheritance rights, unknown to any of the other civilizations of the era, Islam forced the recognition of the juridical rights of women, something that had never previously been done throughout the history of mankind.[1]

Returning to the primary source, the Qur'ān, in search of verses about inheritance rules, one is struck by the following two verses that, alone, sum up the whole philosophy of the Qur'ān on this issue:

> Unto the men a share [*nasīb*] of what parents and kinsfolk leave, and unto the women a share [*nasīb*] of what parents and kinsfolk leave, be it little or much—a share ordained [*nasīban mafrūdan*].[2]
>
> And covet not that by which God has favored some of you above others—unto men a share [*nasīb*] of what they have earned, and unto women a share [*nasīb*] of what they have earned—but ask God of His bounty. Truly God is the Knower of all things.[3]

From these two verses, we see that the Qur'ān establishes a basic rule—the equality of the shares (*nasīb*) allocated to men and women from the inheritance left by their deceased respective parents or relatives. This rule is valid no matter "be it little or much—a share ordained [*nasīban*

---

[1] The 1804 Napoleonic Code established the legal incapacity of married women. In general, Western women did not gain full access to inheritance until the twentieth century.

[2] The Qur'ān 4:7.

[3] Ibid.:32.

mafrūdan]." We note, in passing, the Qur'ān's insistence, at the end of the verse, on the mandatory nature of such equal distribution (*nasīban mafrūdan*).

Before moving further, it would be useful to examine the circumstances of the revelation of these verses—triggering events, context, and the underlying spirit of the revealed verse. In terms of verse 7 of *sūrah* 4, most classic commentators report that it was revealed in response to a request made by a woman named Umm Kuha, reported to having come to the Prophet to lodge a complaint; in her reported words: "my husband has just died and left me with the girls. He left significant assets, which are in the hands of his family. They[4] do not want to give any of it to me or to my daughters, and we are in need."

The Prophet called in the men in question; they freely admitted what was reported by the woman (widow) and justified their refusal to give any part of the inheritance to her and her daughters by the fact that they "do not ride a horse, do not fight against the enemies, and do not carry any loads;" in their eyes, and in accordance with the customs of the time, the women did not have any "return value" and hence should be excluded from the inheritance. The Prophet told them that they will have to wait for the response of the Creator, which did not take long to come, in the form of a verse: "unto men a share [*nasīb*] of what they have earned, and unto women a share [*nasīb*] of what they have earned—but ask God of His bounty. Truly God is the Knower of all things."[5] Thus, this verse came to establish a new legal order in the social fabric of the time by giving women not only a part of the heritage—to which they never had any rights—but also a share that equals that of men.

This is decidedly the verse that establishes equality between men and women in inheritance. The response of the Qur'ān as revealed in this verse, as a result of the complaint of the destitute woman who, furthermore, was responsible for the welfare of her daughters, all of whom were deprived of any of what was left by her departing husband and the father of her children, is a very clear sign of the Qur'ān's determination to do away with the discriminatory customs toward the most disadvantaged, in general, and women, in particular.

---

[4] Suyid and Akrama, respectively, the husband's cousins and a family legal guardian.

[5] Abū al-Hassan an-Nīsābūrī, *Asbāb an-nuzūl*, reviewed and corrected by Sa'īd Mahmūd 'Aqil.

In his commentary on this verse, Ibn Kathīr affirms the following conclusion: "Everyone is on equal footing before this Divine law, and all—men and women—are equal in terms of the core principles of inheritance."[6] Once again, the response, as revealed in the verse, has been to defend the oppressed, the most excluded from society and the most deprived, and pleading their cause.

In all societies, legal systems that are put in place by the ruling elite made sure that only those who are part of the elite group, the rich and the powerful, would benefit from inherited wealth. The oppressed, the underprivileged, the children, the elderly, whether men or women, were excluded, exploited, and relegated to the very bottom of the social order.

Once again, the Qur'ān responds to the demands of women. By means of the intermediary of Umm Kuha's complaint, the distressed cries of all women of this era have been heard by the Creator of the Universe. And the immediate response was the establishment of an equitable access to inheritance for all. And it is not accidental that this verse refers, by name, to men and women, so that there would be no doubt in anyone's mind regarding the fair-mindedness of this distribution. What is more, the Qur'ān made such fair distribution compulsory. Today, these two elements—fairness and compulsion—require even more consideration than before given that the question of inheritance remains to be a part of what we might call the "religious unthinkables" in the land of Islam.

The second verse (4:32) also highlights the same egalitarian distribution of inheritance but also takes into account the labor of men and women during their life on earth. This verse plays a very important role in the affirmation of the economic independence of women by specifically highlighting the labor of both men and women: "unto men a share [*nasīb*] of what they have earned, and unto women a share [*nasīb*] of what they have earned." Formulated in terms of today's context, the principles of this verse correspond to what we call "equal pay for equal work." In fact, as confirmed by Islamic jurisprudence, through this verse and many others, the Qur'ān is very exacting in what concerns the autonomy and financial independence of women. Women, just as men, have the right to manage their own property and commercial affairs and have the power and freedom to conclude sale and purchase contracts, as

---

[6] *Tafsīr Ibn Kathīr*, commentary on verse 7 of *sūrah* 4.

well as the ability to bequeath wills and to establish leases and legal prox-
ies (powers of attorney).

This is also the verse that constitutes the founding Islamic legal principle stipulating, in those cases in which women have total independence
and financial autonomy, that the husband has absolutely no rights to the
revenues or assets of his wife. Regarding the Qur'ānic confirmation of
this basic principle of equality in inheritance, and the economic equality of men and women, commentators report specific historical details
regarding the cause of the revelation of the verse (4:32), details that are
particularly significant in terms of the spiritual and sociocultural elation
in which the Muslims of the time lived.

Thus, according to multiple sources, the verse was revealed on the
occasion of a growing rivalry between men and women. In fact, women
had started to come to the Prophet to complain that men had more
rights than they, as they—the men—were much better recognized and
valued because of their contributions, among others, to armed conquests. The women had therefore expressed their wish to bear arms and
to participate in these conquests in order to enjoy the same benefits that
the men were receiving.[7]

The multiple requests by women to the Prophet include one that is
reported by several commentators and cited by al-Rāzī and others concerning a woman who came to complain to the Prophet, saying: "The
Creator of men and women is one, and you, you are the prophet of
women and men, and our common parents, men or women, are Adam
and Eve, so why does God call only men and does not call us, the
women?"[8] We should note that the content of this demand and others testify to the spirit and intelligence of these women, having been
empowered by the new religion and the force of their own faith. Never
once were they chided or silenced because they were women. We must
also take note of the general freedom of expression that prevailed during this period and the self-assuredness with which women claimed
ownership by exercising it for the first time in their lives. From the way
they expressed themselves, these women appear to have felt "entitled"
to be treated, in terms of both rights and responsibilities, as their kins-
men. And as we have witnessed previously, they did not shy away from

---

[7]There are many versions of this, including one that was reported by Umm Salama, the
wife of the Prophet. Cf. *Tafsīr Ibn Kathīr*, commentary of verse 32 of *sūrah* 4.

[8]Al-Rāzī, *Mafātīḥ al-ghayb*.

being vocal and expecting to be heard, including in mixed assemblies. Undoubtedly, their newly found self-assuredness was greatly facilitated and nurtured by the character of the Prophet—his largesse of spirit, grandeur of mind, forbearance, and strong pedagogical sense—who did everything to guide and encourage them in their first emancipatory steps.

How could all of this have happened and with such openness, over fourteen centuries ago, with women feeling confident to be engaged and to participate in ongoing discourses, raising questions, protesting, when they felt needed, and reaping the fruits of their newly granted freedom when, today, such spaces are in the order of the unthinkable in the vast majority of Muslim communities?

One cannot but be baffled by this wind of freedom that reigned in the era of the Revelation, totally at odds with the current situation in which many Muslim women around the world do not even have access to respectable spaces to pray, in large mosques that appear to have been designed for the service of men and men alone. What is worse is that, today, the great majority of Muslim men and women accept, maybe even believe, that this marginalization of women in the workplace and in religious spaces has been decreed by Islam, that it has always been this way, and hence should not be questioned.

To go back to the consideration of the circumstances of the revelation, as we have seen, this verse followed a number of complaints, most of which from women, but there were also a number of "complaining" men. In fact, the classic commentaries report certain requests made by men who demanded a larger share of the rewards for the simple reason of being men.[9]

The verse was thus revealed at a time of rivalry between men and women, alluded to in the beginning of the verse, "And covet not that by which God has favored some of you above others," with the purpose being putting an end to such rivalry; the prescription that flows from it resulted in the establishment of a basic egalitarian principle that transcends gender and which thus values one criteria—merit. It is not the masculine or the feminine gender that is prime in the evaluation of human beings; it is the efforts of each, their capacity to give, to work, and to strive for the best, in other words, to deploy the necessary internal

---

[9] Cf. *Tafsīr Ibn Kathīr.*

force to attain the moral value that he or she merits. The divine prescription cannot be clearer: Human beings, men and women, will be judged according to the efforts deployed for the good in this world and according to their meritorious efforts, not their origin, gender, or wealth.

Unfortunately, this is not the interpretation shared by many classic commentators, who remained hostages to their own cultural norms and refused to acknowledge gender equality despite the revelation of these verses that make it extremely clear in their formulation.

This is the case of the commentary of al-Rāzī, who affirms: "Men will have a share they have earned with their works, that is, their care and the material support of women; as for the women, their share is to protect their chastity, respect the obedience duty to their husbands, and to assume their household chores and responsibilities such as cooking, baking, and washing clothes."[10] Here, we are very far from the egalitarian principles and objectives affirmed by the verse which does not, at any point, speak, even vaguely, about the duties of women or the charges of a conjugal home, let alone obedience or cooking. What we see here is the usual forceful insistence of the majority of Muslim scholars, including contemporary ones, regarding the question of the wife's duty to obey her husband, which they pull out at every occasion despite the verse itself not even remotely alluding to such an obligation.

This commentary exemplifies, once again, the enormous gap between Qur'ānic principles on the one hand and the different interpretations of classic commentators on the other. One might understand the reasons and the manner in which classic Muslim scholars remained strongly influenced by their sociocultural environment. The problem we are facing today has been generated by a long period of intellectual stagnation and decadence of Islamic thought, following the earlier golden age of the Islamic civilization, which lead to the ratification of the early interpretations of the Qur'ān by succeeding generations of Muslim scholars to the point of making the interpretations appear to be on the order of the sacrosanct, the untouchable. From that point forward, classic-era interpretations remained intact, never having been the object of a contextual study or even a critical examination. Thus, until the present time, they continue unchanged and are designated as absolute truths in lectures given in the main Islamic universities worldwide.

---

[10] Al-Rāzī, op. cit.

In addition to these two verses, which define the egalitarian basis of common inheritance, we find in the Qur'ān many other verses that depict and precisely define the distribution of shares in inheritance. The division of inheritance is essentially based on three criteria, fundamental for the understanding of the Qur'ānic logic that presides over the sharing of inherited property:

1. The degree of kinship of successors to the deceased: Whether men or women, the closer the kinship tie the inheritor has with the deceased, the larger will be his or her share of the inheritance.
2. The position of the generation that inherits: The young generation (men and women) who have just started assuming life's responsibilities are favored over the old generation that is at the end of their lives and who, they themselves, are likely to already be or soon become the responsibility of the young members of the family.
3. The material responsibility incumbent on he who has to be in charge of the material needs of the entire extended family. It is only in this context and within this particular framework that men (brothers) are favored over women (sisters) in terms of inheritance rights, due to their greater financial responsibilities [at that time].

It is essential to keep in mind this fundamental rule in the logic of the Qur'ān in order to understand the reason why, at times, higher shares of inheritance are allocated to some over others. It boils down to the degree of a successor's financial responsibility, combined with his or her kinship proximity to the deceased. This logic follows the same Qur'ānic principle that prioritizes the protection of the most vulnerable in a community or within the structure of a traditional extended family, whereby multiple generations, along with aunts and uncles and their offspring, live together under the same roof, eat from the same pot, and depend on the same purse for their incidental financial needs.

While many, especially in the West, believe that there is only one rule of succession in force in Islam—a woman receiving half a man's share—Islamic inheritance law cannot be reduced to that of half a share for a sister compared to a brother's full share. In fact, there are no less than thirty cases in the Qur'ān where women inherit an equal or even a larger share than that of men.[11] For example, in the case of the death of one of the children, both parents, the mother and father, receive equal shares of the inheritance. The only verse in the Qur'ān that sets the half-a-share rule for girls relates to the case of a sister or sisters inheriting half of the share inherited by a brother or brothers: "God enjoins upon you concerning (the provision for) your children: unto the male a share equal to that of two females; but if there are only daughters, two or more, then unto them is two-thirds of what he leaves; if only one, then unto her a half."[12] Such division, as we have explained earlier, has to do with the continued financial responsibility of brothers regarding the entire family, while sisters are free to dispose of their money and assets as they please. Some explain this distribution saying that the sister receives a "net" amount in addition to her other assets, whereas the brother receives a "gross" amount from which he will have to deduct the expenditures incurred for the maintenance of other household dependents, including the sister who has inherited half his share.[13]

The verse fixing the distribution among siblings at the rate of half a share for the sister was revealed to respond to the socioenvironmental demands of the era to ensure the continuation of the extended family structure via a socially responsible division of family assets so that the brother assumes his responsibility to meet the family's financial needs, including the sister, but also other family members who are unable to care for themselves. In short, the logic of the Qur'ānic division of inheritance must be understood within the then existing framework of family structure, based on the notion of group solidarity. Today, this extended family structure has been replaced by a nuclear family model, one that has neither the form nor the realities that had justified the Qur'ānic distribution logic.

The Qur'ānic allocations were fair and just given the household structure of the era of the Revelation. However, given the nuclear family structure in which we live today—where sisters are rarely financially supported by their brothers and often contribute to the economic well-being of the entire family, including parents and brothers—can we continue to justify the inheritance division rules of bygone era?

[11] Cf. Salāh ad-Dīn's study on women's inheritance in Islam: *Mīrāth al-mar'a wa qadiyyat al-musāwāt* (An-Nahda, 1999).

[12] The Qur'ān 4:11.

[13] Azizah el-Hibri, *Droits des femmes musulmanes dans le village mondial.*

In today's context, not only has the literal application of the verse concerning the division among siblings become a profound structural injustice, it also departs from the stated objectives of the Qur'ān which, as we have seen, advocate the protection and preservation of the assets of women and vulnerable minorities and the fair division of responsibilities within the family.

With the law of inheritance, the Qur'ān has inaugurated a new reign in which the "law" was prime, thereby repealing the rule of discriminatory customs. And it did this by taking into account the socio-cultural benchmarks of the time while simultaneously underscoring the core values of fairness and justice that must always prevail, regardless of the sociocultural context. It is to those first intentions of the Qur'ān that one has to return in order to be able to deal with the challenges that are posed by the current context—baffling, complex, and particularly unjust. So it would be most auspicious at this time of history to return to the verses that define the basis of the general equality in inheritance and to reread them in light of the lessons they convey, along with verses that describe women's half-a-share rule and the logic behind it to determine its continued rationality given where societies stand today in terms of emancipation, evolution, and responsibility, including financial responsibility.

The solution is found in the Qur'ān itself, in particular the fundamental verse that reinforces its egalitarian approach to inheritance: "Unto the men a share [*nasīb*] of what parents and kinsfolk leave, and unto the women a share [*nasīb*] of what parents and kinsfolk leave, be it little or much—a share ordained [*nasīban mafrūdan*]."

The "taboo" that hangs over the ongoing debates in Muslim countries, especially around the question of inheritance among siblings, can be sidestepped if we only knew how to return to the spirit of the Qur'ān and consider this verse as a priority prescription in the inheritance system in Islam.[14] Such an approach would allow us to conduct the debate

---

[14] The inheritance debate takes place in a rather tacit manner in Sunni milieus; paradoxically, in the Islamic Republic of Iran, it has taken place and has evolved. The Iranian parliament passed a law on May 21, 2004, that gives women the same inheritance rights as men. And even though this law has not yet received the approval of the Council of Guardians (of the revolution), it has the merit of showing that such discussion can take place within Islam.

from within an Islamic framework while remaining true to its ethical foundations.

The Qur'ān provides us with the proof that nothing is definitive or closed forever; on the contrary, in each context, we should know how to put the main goals of the spiritual message, including the first principle of justice that represents one of the structural elements, forward. A return to this central and vital verse on inheritance is to contribute to keeping the spirit of Islam alive in the hearts of Muslims within today's socioeconomic realities.

CHAPTER 14

Foundations of Corporal Ethic

In the West as in the East, in the North as in the South, the body and standardized corporal norms have today become the center of attention in terms of questions of ethics and morality. The dictates of physical appearance are now among the most important socioeconomic and cultural markers of modernity. Needless to say, these sociocultural norms of appearance are much more focused on women, whose bodies have become an important subject of graphic representations, carefully nurtured by the media, but also and most importantly by skillful marketing strategists for the highest effectiveness and returns, at all levels.

Much more than ever before, modernity is now defined by women's bodies, transformed, by the force of circumstances, into a real battlefield where the various dominant ideologies will compete and clash. There is a recurrent visual representation of women in the advertising landscape that borders indecency and reflects a true "commodification" of the body through sponsored and excessively commoditized images. This leads to the erection of yet another barrier for those who struggle for the empowerment and liberation of women, further challenged by the broadly publicized images of women, fabricated by a market ideology that glorifies eternal youth, worships physical beauty, and reduces the feminine ideal to a single aesthetic dimension.

The empowerment of women has certainly settled a certain number of problems in relation to the rights of women, including that of financial independence and autonomy; it is clear, however, that the "liberation of mores," claimed by many feminist movements, was incapable of

© The Author(s) 2018
A. Lamrabet, *Women and Men in the Qur'ān*,
https://doi.org/10.1007/978-3-319-78741-1_14

dismantling the traditional relationship of seduction that has, for centuries, governed human relations and provided the background against which each setting developed its own means of resistance. In hypermodern societies, this relationship of seduction also responds to the same balance of power because women remain the inveterate objects of the representation of a dominant and omnipresent male desire.

Concerning this relationship with the body, Eastern and Western societies exalt the same image, even though this is done via different cultural registers, one being the image of the hyper-sexed body, eternally young, exploitable to the utmost, and handed over for public view in the greater consumer market. Paradoxically, it is in countries where longstanding cultural traditions limit the visibility of women's bodies that this consumer market and body imaging is often most pronounced.[1] It is also in the same societies, in parallel with body worship and a focus on physical appearance, that we find the most traditionalist Islamic discourse and rhetoric and the strictest disciplinarians regarding the female dress code. Indeed, these discourses convey, in general, a codified image of corpse and dress codes that boil down to an exaggerated focus on women's bodies, perceived as the "custodians of the honor" of Islam and Muslims.

In other words, in parallel with what appears to be a genuine ideology of the worship of the body in hyperglobalized modern cultures that exploits women's bodies and controls their images, while giving them the impression of being liberated, there is an almost identical body-focused logic within contemporary Islamic cultural ideologies that, in the name of Islam, seeks to confine women's bodies in clothes that follow a certain dress code that is, supposedly, in compliance with *Shari'a*, referred to as *al-Libās ash-Shar'ī* (clothing compliant with Islamic law).

We can thus recognize in the contemporary Islamic discourse a dominant trend that compresses the entire Islamic corporal ethic into narrowly defined conduct that is focused principally on women. In short, the debate around the corporal ethic, or should we say the dress ethic, in Islam revolves around a single feature, that of the *hijāb* or veil that must be worn by Muslim women. Furthermore, the term *hijāb*, which as we shall see is completely inappropriate, symbolizes in the collective

---

[1] The consumption of cosmetics and perfume in the Gulf States (UAE) is among the highest in the world, according to *Gulf News* (April 16, 2016). While Saudi Arabia leads the overall sales market in the Middle East and Africa ($5.3 billion in 2015), per capita consumption is the highest in the UAE ($239 in 2015).

imagination of many Muslims the fundamental criterion underpinning the entire mass of Islamic conduct in relation to the body. Today, speaking of the relationship between Islam and body ethics brings us back to the subject of the so-called Islamic veil that women use and which has become, due to the bombardment of ideological forces, the symbol of Islam, its identity, and its ongoing resistance to moral decadence, presumed to be exclusively intrinsic to Western cultures. Obviously, this is completely wrong, since all societies, to varying degrees, possess their share of moral and social decay.

But what does the Qur'ān say about this subject? And what are the foundations of corporal and dress ethic in the Qur'ān?

THE ETHIC OF INWARDNESS

Using the holistic approach to Qur'ānic text, in reference to the Qur'ānic ethic relative to the body and dress (*libās*), one finds the following verse that seems central to an evaluation of this ethic: "O Children of Adam! We have indeed sent down upon your raiment [*libās*] to cover your nakedness, and rich adornment [*rīsh*]. But the raiment of reverence [*libās at-taqwā*], that is better. This is among the signs of God, that haply they may remember."[2] This verse that addresses all human beings, men, and women, consecutively describes three types of attire: The first is that which protects the nudity of human beings; the second is that which embellishes and beautifies (*rīsh*); the third is described in the Qur'ān as that of "interiority" or "inwardness" (*libās at-taqwā*).

The first type of attire corresponds to that which is meant to "cover" the nudity of human beings. Isn't hiding one's nakedness one of the first rules of human morality? The Qur'ān recalls a gesture as old as humanity itself to mind, a desire to hide nudity that generates an instinctive uneasiness of being undressed, "a nudity that expresses discomfort, humiliation and dissonance, rather than wellbeing."[3] This nudity, an expression of human unease, is in fact mentioned in the history of Adam and Eve, who become aware of their nakedness following their disobedience of the Creator, which earned them eviction from Paradise. Beyond the material expression of nudity, as such, it is also about the exposure of

[2] The Qur'ān 7:26.

[3] André Guindon, *L'habillé et le nu. Pour une éthique du vêtir et du denuder* (University of Ottawa Press, 2014).

their moral weakness, their faults and their human imperfections: "Thus he lured them on through deception. And when they tasted of the tree, their nakedness was exposed to them and they began to sew together the leaves of the Garden to cover themselves. And their Lord called out to them, 'Did I not forbid you from that tree and tell you that Satan is a manifest enemy unto you.'"[4]

The second attire described by the Qur'ān is that of embellishments/adornments (*rīsh*), a term that, for the Arabs of the era, designated everything related to beauty and ornamentation. The commentator, Ibn 'Abbās, interprets the term *rīsh* in the sense of wealth and affluence.[5] The distinction made in the Qur'ān between "clothing" and "adornment," two gifts that God bestowed on humans, constitutes an effective approval by the Qur'ān of a sartorial gesture that combines beauty and refinement. "God is beautiful and loves beauty," as stated in a *hadīth*.[6]

The Qur'ān reminds humans that the attributes of beauty and wealth are not contrary to the practice of spiritual requirements; neither is austerity and deprivation necessarily synonymous with religious devotion. The beauty of which the Qur'ān speaks can effectively be both internal and external, and the appreciation and attachment to the beautiful things in life is absolutely not in contradiction to a heart containing faith and love for the Creator. A *hadīth* recounts: "God loves to see his blessings reflected in the lifestyle and the way in which his believers dress."[7]

The tradition of the Prophet of Islam reinforces the idea that spirituality can be expressed through some elegance of mind and body. The Prophet was always careful that he presented himself appropriately to visitors, companions, and relatives, both in terms of his physical appearance and attire and his conduct—his courtesy and respect for others. The beauty and elegance that knows how to present itself, in harmony and finesse, are gifts from God, and what the Qur'ān teaches through the ethics of *libās* (attire).

As the Qur'ān makes very clear, *libās at-taqwā* is the finest of all and that which God prefers: "But the raiment of reverence [*libās at-taqwā*], that is better. This is among the signs of God, that haply they may

---

[4] Cf. The Qur'ān 7:21–22 and 20:121.

[5] *Tafsīr Ibn Kathīr.*

[6] An authenticated *hadīth*, reported by Muslim.

[7] An authenticated *hadīth*, reported by at-Tirmīdī.

remember" (7:26). Many meanings have been given to this Qur'ānic expression, *libās at-taqwā*, by the early classic commentators. Ibn 'Abbās, for example, interprets it as "good deeds" (*al-'amal as-sālih*). Others have spoken of good appearance, dignity, modesty, virtue, purity, integrity, humility, and respect.[8] Some Muslim scholars say that *libās at-taqwā* is the attire that never wears out because it represents the "beauty of the heart and soul."[9]

These different interpretations are strengthened by the following saying by the Prophet: "God does not look at your physical appearance, nor your material wealth; he is more interested in your heart and soul." In itself, this *hadīth* summarizes the deeper meaning of this Qur'ānic recommendation of *libās at-taqwā*, which is the best attire in the eyes of God.

This distinction between exterior and interior attire is the very foundation of the Qur'ān regarding the manner in which humans dress. What matters is not so much what you wear—its value or how it looks—but the degree of sincerity or integrity in the deepest parts of our interior. So, whatever one may do to improve his or her appearance, it is our "inwardness" that will be reflected in the eyes of others. The preservation of a degree of decorum in dress that conceals one's nudity is a basic principle of corporal ethics. Adorning oneself with beautiful and valuable clothes, without arrogance or indecency, is to accept God's divine generosity. But to adorn oneself with *libās at-taqwā* is to achieve spiritual perfection in the eyes of the Creator because, incontestably, it is the "attire within" that is judged by God as the best of all.

This verse thus motivates people to adopt a manner of dressing that, while paying attention to detail and beauty, remains true to an interior that reflects, all at once, the respect, dignity, modesty, and sincerity of the soul. It is this harmony of the senses and the soul—a subtle balance between the exterior and the interior, the body and the soul—that summarizes the fundamentals of Qur'ānic ethic in reference to one's attire.

---

[8] *Tafsīr Ibn Kathīr.*
[9] Ibid.

THE DEONTOLOGY OF RESPECT OF THE OTHER

After having addressed the general principles of attire, the Qur'ān recommends to men and women believers a series of attitudes related to the ethics of human conduct, as we see in the following verse: "Tell the believing men to lower their eyes [*yaghuddū min absārihim*] and guard their private parts. That is purer for them [*yahfadhū furūjahum*]. Surely God is Aware of whatsoever they do. And tell the believing women to lower their eyes [*yaghudna min absārihinna*] and guard their private parts [*yahfadhna furūjahunna*]."[10] This verse appears repetitive because it reiterates the same ethical principles in connection with the manner in which one "looks" or "gazes" (at others) and sexuality. The Qur'ān reaffirms its commands by calling both men and women separately but equally.

The first Qur'ānic command calls for an action that is referred to in Arabic as *ghadd al-basar*, often interpreted by most commentators as "dropping a part of one's gaze." Such a gesture is taken as a sign of modesty, or bashfulness, vis-à-vis people of the opposite sex, especially since it is closely connected to the following injunction calling for *hifdh al-farj*, which means chastity in the sense of self-control. These two injunctions are reminders of the important role that a "look" plays in the relations between men and women, a look that is closely related to "chastity," understood as a virtue of restraint. It is evident that these verses are addressed to men and women who live side by side, live together, or share the same activities in the public sphere and in their respective communities.

The spiritual message here addresses a universal theme in the history of humanity, that of the body and the entire philosophy of pleasure, the desire of another, and the physical relations between women and men. These verses sketch the broad outlines of a "manner" that goes beyond appearances but, above all, expresses itself through the eyes, often a decisive determinant of the quality of the relationship of one to another.

The Qur'ān urges people to "lower their eyes" as, above all, a gesture of respect toward the other person. To "lower the gaze" is therefore to know how to keep the right balance between interest, expressed in the "look," and "reserve and restraint," generated by respect. This is an attempt to recognize the other—the one we look at and address—first

---

[10] The Qur'ān 24:30–31.

and foremost for his or her humanity, thus exceeding the limits imposed by a passing look or a sustained look that only sees the exterior of the body.

The second injunction, a consequence of the "look" ethic, is *hifdh al-farj*, an expression that is often translated as "chastity." This attitude must, however, be understood as a "regulation of sexuality." In Islam, as in other religious traditions, it is not an issue of "slighting" the body and sexuality, nor is it strictness or abstinence in the ascetic sense. Sexuality in Islam is permitted only in the framework of marriage, in other words, in a committed and responsible relationship; therefore, the injunction is rather to develop the ability to control human impulses and to maintain a good balance between the spiritual and the carnal.

These two Qur'ānic principles, the "gaze" ethic and the control of desires are therefore closely interlinked. In fact, these two aspects have been reconciled by some contemporary Christian theologians who have addressed the question of chastity through the gaze:

> The modest gaze supports distance and respect of the otherness (which cannot be reduced to the difference). It sees the body as personal and expressive before seeing it as object of desire. ... Chastity is freedom or, more precisely, freedom vis-à-vis the desire. The difficulty that we have of placing an innocent glance on a naked body is certainly a sign of access to modesty, that is to say, the sense of intimacy, but also the limits of the unification within us of desire and freedom. The notion of purity of vision would be to rediscover, in connection with the purity of heart.[11]

It is the path of freedom that the Qur'ānic message is calling us toward—the freedom to remain who and what we are, through the eyes of others, but also to remain respectful of the interiority of the other as we pass a glance, for respecting the other, before all, is an act of self-respect. These notions of modesty, of moderation, and of respect for the body and the privacy of the other are of paramount importance today, invaded by a culture that passionately "sanctifies" the body and physical pleasure and, through excessive libertinism, trivializes the spread of sexual violence, especially among the younger generations. In fact, a good number of social scientists are troubled by the resurgence of sexual stereotypes and the impact of invasive sexualization of the public space on the

---

[11] Xavier Lacroix, *Le corps de chair* (Cerf, 1992), p. 88.

thought processes and behavior, especially the young.[12] We should also learn how to stay within the golden mean, as taught by the Qur'ān, and not be carried away by extreme rigorousness that confuses modesty and prudishness and regards any relationship between men and women as the starting point of inevitable moral deviation. The spiritual message here seeks that men and women believers learn a proper relational ethic, one that is sound and balanced, in other words, the humanization of their relations.

Unfortunately, this is not the approach followed by the classic Islamic discourse that gives the impression that all relations between men and women are "suspect" until they are proven to be otherwise. This is an extreme vision that reduces the bulk of relational ethics between men and women to a fairly limited, even archaic, notion of "modesty," which coincides with the modesty of access or excessive modesty.

This virtue of modesty (bashfulness), according to the same discourse, becomes an "obligation" that is incumbent only on women. And with some of them, it would even be a quality attributable exclusively to women because they are suspected to be the source of all temptations. Now, modesty, in its larger Qur'ānic sense, is the valuation of the respect of the privacy of the other and of oneself; and it is a Qur'ānic value that challenges both men and women, without distinction. The Prophet affirms that "modesty is part of faith." And one of the traits that characterized the Prophet was his deep modesty.

The Prophet of Islam has also demonstrated the magnitude of this notion of modesty, in his encouragement of male and female believers constantly to assume the demeanor of true modesty when they are facing the Creator: "Be modest with respect to God, as it should be," he recommended,[13] so that they know how to preserve the posture of respect and compliance with the spiritual principles dictated by God.

Modesty in its Qur'ānic sense is not a restrictive notion only in its carnal dimension or in reference to human relations, especially between men and women. Neither does it suggest submissiveness or the effacement or the annulment of one's personality. However, this notion of modesty is sometimes so flawed that it becomes synonymous with

---

[12] Cf. Mariette Julien, *La mode hypersexualisée, une mode controversée* (Sisyphe 2010). In this work, the author expresses her concern at seeing girls "transformed into objects of desire when they do not yet have the capacity to be subjects of desire."

[13] A *hadīth* transmitted by Ibn Mas'ūd and reported by Ahmad.

social hypocrisy and a source of a double-edged morality. This eventually results in the distortion of human relations, especially that between men and women, which, above all, must be based on respect and mutual consideration. True modesty, as the Qur'ān teaches us, is the value of respect, of moderation. Such modesty can only be generated by souls that are at peace with themselves in their spirituality and in their faith. And we need to know how to revive such virtue that has become obsolete by returning to its original sense. We should also assert the right to an ethic of modesty, especially today when our natural modesty is continually assaulted by a universal culture of voyeurism and immodesty which we, ironically, tend to accept as if they were intrinsic to modernity and individual freedoms.

Beyond Attire

A verse from the Qur'ān speaks of a certain type of attire that is called *jilbāb*: "O Prophet! Tell thy wives and thy daughters, and the women of the believers to draw their cloaks [*jilbāb*] over themselves (when they go out). Thus it is likelier that they will be known and not be disturbed."[14] In Arabic, the term *jilbāb* designates any item of clothing that is worn over clothes, similar to a trench coat or a cape, or, in the tradition of Arabia, a long thin overcoat referred to as *'abāya*.

In terms of the circumstances of the revelation of this verse, most classic commentators agree that it was revealed in response to a real-life experience of some Muslim women who were assaulted by young men in the dark alleys of Medina, when they went to the mosque to perform their night or dawn prayers.[15] Some other commentators affirm that this verse was revealed in order to distinguish between free and slave women. In other words, the *jilbāb* was to be worn only by free women so that they be recognized and thus not assaulted while out at night. Thus, according to this interpretation, the *jilbāb*, worn only by free elite women, becomes an indicator of "social distinction" that protects them from possible attacks. This type of logic strongly implies that slave women did not have any rights, hence subject to being assaulted without this being morally reprehensible.

---

[14] The Qur'ān 33:59.
[15] Zamakhsharī, *Tafsīr al-kashshāf*.

This type of interpretation, in addition to its lack of coherence, does not in the least correspond with the global ethic taught by the spiritual message of Islam, which is, as we have seen, particularly resolute in its insistence on the maintenance of a spirit of social justice. How can such a creed accept to favor some women over others? And how could the Qur'ān prescribe the liberation of slaves, whether men or women, and consider such action as a profound act of piety and then, at the same time, perpetuate this type of distinction—social discrimination?

Some contemporary Muslim scholars have challenged this type of interpretation, affirming that this verse concerned all women of the era, whether free or slaves.[16] In fact, the verse does not make reference to any distinction between free and slave women. Rather, the object of the verse is to call all the women of the era and to advise them to wear the *jilbāb* to protect themselves from the harassment they were clearly victims of at that time. Hence, this attire prescription should be looked at in light of the happenings at the time. Therefore, in no way should it be generalized or given a universal scope because it remains tied to specific and circumstantial events during the era in which the first Muslim community was being erected.

Nevertheless, one should bear in mind the timelessness of the original intent of this verse—the protection of vulnerable minorities, including women, be they free or slaves. In that sense, this verse is part of the aim of the Qur'ān: the protection of the most vulnerable. What is worth noting here is that, while the Qur'ān wanted to protect women from aggressors, it did not forbid them from leaving their homes at night, to go to the mosque, despite the risks they were facing. So, rather than stopping with the imposition of attire supposedly meant for free elite women, this—the protection of women, including their liberty of movement—is what matters the most and should be retained regarding this verse. The Qur'ān has encouraged women, all women, whatever their social status might have been, to be present everywhere, even during evening prayers in the mosque, which was, at that time, the sociopolitical meeting point of the nascent Muslim community.

Despite the risks they would face, it was important for the Qur'ān to preserve the presence of women in the mosque, alongside men, hence advising them, temporarily, to protect themselves by following the dress

---

[16]Cf. Sheikh Sayyid at-Tantāwi, *Al-wasīt fī tafsīr al-qur'ān al-karīm.*

custom of the time. Thus, the priority for the Qur'ān was the education of the community about equality despite the cultural prejudices against women and despite the fact that their presence in the streets of Medina and at the mosque of the Prophet, at night, was something socially unacceptable at the time.

Unfortunately, this is not the understanding that the interpreters of the Qur'ān were going to disseminate, as they were not able to incorporate, culturally speaking, this divine pedagogy of equality between men and women. This is something we see through their successive interpretations and the cultural reality of successive Muslim societies that will curb this Qur'ānic liberation movement by "reinstating" social distinctions and the confinement of women in harems and other seraglios. All designs to prevent women from gaining access to public spaces will now be legitimate; the smallest social conflict, the smallest *fitna* (discord) will serve as an occasion to ban the presence of women in the Muslim sociopolitical sphere—prohibitions that will "naturally" be justified in the name of Islam, even though it is radically contrary to the egalitarian spirit of the Qur'ān such as the one expressed once again in this verse.

THE SO-CALLED ISLAMIC VEIL: *KHIMĀR* OR *HIJĀB*?

Right now, whether in Muslim countries or in the West, the *hijab*, or veil, has become a most controversial subject, generating behavior akin to mass hysteria, and interlocking, in a rather puzzling fashion, notions as diverse as tradition, modernity, freedom, the female body, identity, and the challenge of living together in multicultural societies. The debate has also brought about the "unveiling" of two important issues of our time, one in the West, and the other in Muslim countries. In the West, the veil has led to the growing visibility of Muslims which, in turn, has brought into focus debates about the place of Islam in societies that are, themselves, in an identity restructuring phase. In Muslim countries, the issue of the veil has confirmed the existence of a profound identity crisis, illustrated by the intensity of the emotional load surrounding this emblem, the veil, which has come to symbolize and encapsulate the essence of Muslim identity.

To best understand the significance and implications of the veil in Islam, we need to go beyond the issue itself—the right to wear or not to wear the veil, and its religious legitimacy or illegitimacy—and return to the source—the Qur'ānic text—to see how the sacred has addressed the subject: the actual terminology used and the significance such terminology imparts regarding the ethic and code of the "proper" attire for women in Islam. It would be important to highlight, at the outset, that the usually used term, *hijāb*, does not in the least correspond to what it is in reference to, namely, the headscarf that covers the hair of some Muslim women when in public. Nowhere in the Qur'ān is the term *hijāb* ascribed with that particular meaning. One can in fact say that, both in terms of its semantic and conceptual interpretation, the term *hijāb* rather embodies the opposite of what it is supposed to mean.

The Term *Hijāb* in the Qur'ān

The term *hijāb* is mentioned seven times in the Qur'ān, always with the same meaning, which is not the case with many other words that are, at times, polysemantic. The word *hijāb* means "curtain," "separation," "partition"; in other words, the thing that hides and conceals an object, whether a thing or human. In French, this notion corresponds to the term "voile," that which protects and masks something. The synonym of *hijāb* in Arabic is *sitr*, which means the thing that separates, such as a wall, a screen, or any other virtual separation. One finds this term—*hijāb*—used in the following verses:

> And when thou recitest the Qur'ān, We place a hidden veil [*hijāb*] between thee and those who believe not in the Hereafter.[17]
>
> It is not for any human being that God should speak unto him, save by revelation, or from behind a veil [*hijāb*], or that He should send a messenger in order to reveal what He will by His leave. Truly He is Exalted, Wise.[18]

But the verse that has been most often used as a proof that the "veiling" of women is an "obligation," in Islam, in which the word *hijāb*[19] is used, is the following:

[17] The Qur'ān 17:45.

[18] Ibid. 42:51.

[19] The term *hijāb* is used in the Qur'ān in the following verses 7:46; 17:45; 19:17; 38:32; 41:5; 42:51; 33:53.

O you who believe! Enter not the dwellings of the Prophet for a meal without waiting for its time to come, unless leave be granted you. But if you are invited, enter; and when you have eaten, disperse. Linger not, seeking discourse. Truly that would affront the Prophet, and he would shrink from telling you, but God shrinks not from the truth. And when you ask anything of [his wives], ask them from behind a veil [hijāb].[20]

This verse was revealed at the wedding of the Prophet with Zaynab Bint Jahsh. On this occasion, the Prophet was keen on inviting a large number of people to a dinner party organized in his small home. The tradition reports that, after the meal, three men lingered until very late at night to continue a discussion among themselves, even though the only people who were left there, in addition to the lingering three men, were the Prophet, accompanied by his new bride. Being extremely courteous, the Prophet could not excuse himself to these guests but nevertheless found the situation to be awkward; the revelation of this verse was a way of bringing him a sort of relief.[21]

Some commentaries that support the same narrative regarding the cause and purpose of the revelation, agree that this verse was revealed to instruct believers of the era to respect the privacy of others, particularly that of the Prophet, and to know, in reference to an invitation, when and how to take leave of the host. Other commentators bring to one's attention the presence of the other wives of the Prophet at the ceremony, including Aïsha and the new bride, all eating at the same table as the other guests, as was the practice, to the exasperation of the Prophet's companion, 'Umar Ibn al-Khattāb (became the second Rashidun caliph), known for his rigor and conservatism. It is reported that out of respect for the wives of the Prophet, and in order to shield them from the eyes of visiting strangers who came to the house to see the Prophet, Ibn al-Khattāb has, on a number of occasions, advised the Prophet to hang a curtain (hijāb) that would separate the wives' quarters from the rest of the house.[22]

It is evident, therefore, that the verse was revealed for educational purposes to preserve the intimacy of others but first of all of the Prophet who, because of his specific status of Messenger of God, was entitled to

---

[20] The Qur'ān 33:53.

[21] Cf. Tafsīr Ibn Kathīr and that of al-Qurtubī concerning this verse.

[22] Cf. Tafsīr of al-Qurtubi.

special respect and privacy. This event (and the verse) also served to confirm the special status of "Mothers of Believers," attributed to the wives of the Prophet, to be respected and honored by all members of the community.[23] Thus, the *hijāb*—as a sort of a storefront, not as attire—only concerns the wives of the Prophet and responds to a conjectural necessity for the era to preserve the privacy of the Prophet and his wives within his own home. In short, at no level does the term *hijāb* refer to or even suggest a type of attire or a particular dress code. As mentioned previously, the spirit of this prescription was the teaching of the Arabs of the era the rules of good manners in terms of respecting the privacy of others.

It should also be noted that the *hijāb*, as it was confirmed in this period, does not in the least mean "shutting up" the wives of the Prophet in a secluded area or to isolate them from their environment. The wives of the Prophet themselves did not understand it as such either, as they continued to go about their business as they wished. For example, this prescription certainly did not prevent Aïsha from traveling, accomplishing the pilgrimage, or continuing to receive, even after the death of the Prophet, his companions but also other Muslim scholars from distant lands who traveled to see her in pursuit of her vast knowledge of religion.[24]

It is therefore clear that the term *hijāb* does not in the least correspond with the meaning it has been given, that of a headscarf. And the *hijāb* has absolutely nothing to do with any Islamic attire for women. As we have seen, this is a symbol of the separation between the public and private life during the time of the Prophet, the purpose of which was the consecration of the wives of the Prophet as "Mothers of Believers."

THE HEADSCARF MENTIONED IN THE QUR'ĀN

It is in another Qur'ānic verse in which one finds the word that, in terms of its exact meaning, corresponds with a headscarf:

> And tell the believing women to lower their eyes and to guard their private parts, and to not display their adornment [*zīnatahunna*] except that which is visible thereof. And let them draw their kerchiefs [*khumurihinna*] over their breasts [*juyūbihinna*], and not to display their adornment except

---

[23] Cf. Ibn 'Ashūr, *at-tahrīr wa at-tanwīr*, commentary on this verse.

[24] See Asma Lamrabet, *Aïsha, épouse du Prophète ou l'islam au féminin.*

to their husbands, or their fathers, or their husbands' fathers, or their sons, or their husbands' sons, or their brothers, or their brothers' sons, or their sisters' sons, or their women, or those whom their right hands possess, or male attendants free of desire, or children who are innocent of the private areas of women.[25]

It is this Qur'ānic verse—and not that which speaks of *hijāb*—that specifies some "aspects" of dressing for women believers, including in particular the wearing of a headscarf. The term *khumur* (plural of *khimār*) mentioned in this verse means not only the scarf that the women of the Arabian Peninsula wore but also all other women from other civilizations at that time. The Qur'ān invites women believers to bind off the borders of their scarves/shawls (*khimār*) on their chests to conceal the top of their busts when they leave their homes.

In fact, classic commentaries report that Arab women of Mecca, upon leaving their homes, were accustomed to folding the borders of their shawls/scarves behind their necks, in other words, leaving the throat and the upper chest uncovered, whence the Qur'ānic injunction inviting women believers to bind off the borders of their scarves to cover their chests. The Qur'ān also tells women believers not to show off their beauty and ornaments except for what shows naturally, in other words, which normally stays visible. In terms of the expression "that which is apparent," Ibn 'Abbās specifies that it is in reference to the face and hands of a woman. And this understanding corresponds with the interpretation that most commentators and scholars have followed: Women believers should cover their hair with a *khimār* and show only their face and hands. The verse also seems rather explicit because it stipulates that women should not "show their finery," except in the presence of men with whom they have a direct kinship relationship. In fact, the end of the verse cites, in a rather exhaustive manner, a list of men in the presence of whom women may show their fineries, including their fathers, fathers-in-law, brothers, nephews, etc.

Some scholars of the Hanbali school maintain that women should cover themselves entirely, including the face and the hands, which must be hidden because they are a part of a woman's fineries, as described by the Qur'ān. It is also the same school that prescribes the *Niqāb* or *Burqa* and considers the entire body of a woman "unlawful" to be seen.

---

[25] The Qur'ān 24:31.

Such a position cannot be drawn from the Qur'ān, in which the verse on the *khimār* is clear and does not provide any more details concerning the manner of dressing that Muslim women must adopt. The practice they are prescribing is essentially cultural and dovetails with the traditions of some regions of Arabia where people remain faithful to their ancestral dressing manners.

It would not be futile to mention here that to cover the faces of women would be equivalent to abandoning a Qur'ānic prescription, namely that of *ghadh al-basar* (lowering one's gaze), as there would be no sense in recommending compliance with this ethic of the gaze, as the Qur'an does, if the face is entirely covered. Another proof that reinforces the viewpoint that the *Niqāb*, the cultural origin of which is pre-Islamic, has no Qur'ānic origin is the *hadīth* that forbade the veiling of the face during the pilgrimage and in the sacred precincts of the *Ka'ba*, in contradiction to the assertion of the advocates and followers of the "full veil" notion that they want to legitimize and enforce in the name of Islam.

BETWEEN *HIJĀB* AND *KHIMĀR*: A FORTUITOUS SEMANTIC SHIFT?

Now that we know the distinction between a *hijāb* and a *khimār*, is there a logic behind the stubborn insistence of millions of people around the world to use the term *hijāb* to discuss or describe what we know is a *khimār* and what the Qur'ān itself has called *khimār*? It is indeed astonishing to see the high degree to which this semantic confusion has become all-encompassing and internalized in Muslim societies and communities everywhere, from the learned elite to the common man, passing through academics. All, virtually without exception, incorrectly use the term *hijāb* to describe an item that, etymologically, should be called *khimār*.

Having become so widespread, this semantic error is now almost impossible to rectify. For one thing—despite the reigning confusion— there does not seem to be a strong desire to correct the error. Some may even argue that this error is in the order of negligible; thus, it would be absurd to dispense energy to rectify it when its use has been pervasive and tacitly accepted by all. However, given the extent of the damage caused by the sterile debates around the theme of the *hijāb* and the resulting confusion that governs the minds, it is becoming increasingly urgent, at a minimum, to draw attention to this issue, which can be difficult to resolve unless we are able to deconstruct its surrounding ideological edifice, developed by Muslim literature.

Largely, the blunder we live today is, in most cases, not affected deliberately and remains subconsciously recreated and replicated. On the other hand, the origin of this semantic shift, throughout the history of Islamic thought, is neither innocent nor fortuitous. In general, the shift in meaning is the result of incorrect interpretations and translations that conform to certain sociocultural imperatives in the names of which, at certain moments in history, one attempts to forge "custom-made" concepts in conjunction with an established political order. And this is precisely what happened with the compulsory *hijāb*, imposed, at all costs, on Muslim women, and intentionally incorporating it in the "register" of corporal ethics in Islam. When we go back to the origin and the meaning of the word *hijāb*—to conceal, shield, or separate—and see the transformation process it has undergone, to become a "headscarf," one cannot but wonder if the "double meaning" or "doubling the meaning" of the word *hijāb* had not been executed deliberately in order to be able to justify, religiously speaking, the confinement of Muslim women.

The *hijāb*, in its sense of separation, has been imposed on Muslim women, intentionally sending them the signal concerning their "placement" in society, in other words, to confine them, in the name of Islam, to the shadow, and to push them away from the sociopolitical sphere.

So, replacing the *khimār* with the *hijāb* is the inversion of different, perhaps even opposing, semantic, and conceptual fields to endorse and validate, in the name of Islam, the confinement of women behind a curtain and to exclude them from the sociopolitical space. Indeed, the replacement of the *khimār* by the *hijāb* is confounding two very different registers with one another. While the *khimār* incontestably remains, according to the Qur'ānic vision, a sign of the social visibility of women, namely their active social participation, the *hijāb* marks the relegation of women to the private and intimate sphere. Thus, by analogy, the *hijāb* becomes the symbol of the confinement of the body of women in the interior of the sphere of *fitna* (temptation, seduction) and *'awra*, synonymous to impudence and shame. And it is in the interior of these two concepts of *fitna* and *'awra*, the tangible "collateral effects" of *hijāb*—mind you, a word that does not appear anywhere in the Qur'ān to signify the "forced" meaning—that Muslim women would be confined and eternally condemned throughout the history of Islamic civilization.

Given the absence of any evidence of a confusion between the two concepts of *khimār* and *hijāb* during the time of the Revelation and the very initial period of Islamic civilization, it would be interesting to try to determine the precise moment at which this conceptual substitution of *khimār* and *hijāb* took place by searching through Islamic discourse and jurisprudence.

After the revelation of the particular verse, the early Muslim women who opted for the *khimār* in its Qur'ānic sense did it deliberately and in confirmation of their newly attained freedom. By wearing the *khimār* or a shawl/headscarf, mentioned in the Qur'ān, they also asserted their freedom from the discriminatory traditions that devalued women socially.

The verses related to the dress ethic of women, including that which talks of the *khimār*, should be reread alongside those that give Muslim women the right to economic independence, inheritance, the freedom to choose a husband, and the right to social and political participation. In subscribing to the prescription of *khimār*, the first Muslim women understood it as an integral part of a profound message of liberation and as a symbol of dignity, at long last gained. Therefore, for anyone who desires to understand the profound sense of these verses must first know and contemplate this global conception of the spirit of the Qur'ān and the holistic orientation of its spiritual message. Needless to say, it is not the *khimār*, in and of itself, that is important. It is the new sense that this article of clothing, known long before the advent of Islam, has taken roots and the context within which such action happened—a movement for the liberation of women.

Notwithstanding the intentions of the *khimār*—an article of clothing that facilitated women's participation alongside men in the sociopolitical public arena, thus regarded as a symbol of liberation—it gradually started being referred to, known, and functioning as a *hijāb*—a barrier, a concealer. So, while the referenced article of clothing—scarf or headscarf—remained the same, the function of such article was radically transformed, from a "liberator" into a "separator," from "inclusion" into "exclusion."

The sanctification of the *hijāb* and, at the same time, the virtual removal of the term *khimār* from Islamic vocabulary, has been followed by the invention of a new social code that sanctions, as Islamic, the separation of men and women. The *hijāb*—translated as "veil" in all languages—shall henceforth be established as an emblem of Islam, by means of the female body that finds itself "veiled" and marginalized in the corners of history, to safeguard the patriarchal structures that had initially been weakened by the liberating message of the Qur'ān.

This phenomenon is common to all religious traditions in which the veil, reduced to its etymological sense of "hiding," became an indispensable tool of submission of women to the patriarchal order. In Muslim societies, through the "veiling" of women, all their rights acquired with the advent of Islam would be usurped; the "veil," as with *hijāb*, will represent, in itself, the powerful indicator of the deterioration of the legal status of women in Muslim land, because, in the name of this symbol, she will be cloistered, excluded from the public space, from the rest of the world, excluded from her entire life. Totally invisible, the "veiled" woman behind a *hijāb*, imposed by the law of men and not of God, shall become, paradoxically, the only visible image of an Islam in decadence.

On the political front, the confusion between *hijāb* and *khimār* is subtle and serves the interests of differing ideologies, represented just as much by the adherents of official Islamic states as by radical Muslims, without forgetting the new scholars of modern Islamophobia. While they differ, everyone among them is delighted with setting up the "veil" or the *hijāb* as a banner of Islam, whether to defend or to vilify. Deep down, it is the same logic of exclusion that motivates them all.

CONCLUSION

We have seen the precise way in which the Qur'ān has transmitted its ethical orientation regarding the human body, addressing itself to women and men, without distinction, except for the two verses that speak of *khimār* and *hijāb*. Furthermore, the two verses are also the only verses in the Qur'ān that evoke the dress ethic but without entering into any of the secondary details that one now finds in the books that are targeted to "practicing Muslim women."

Unfortunately, the entire Qur'ānic ethic seems to have been reduced to the dressing manner of women, and only women—their bodies, the precise way in which they should be covered, the color and thickness of the cloth, and the uniformity of the attire—in total disregard of the Qur'ān's message of "dressing," as expressed in the three verses, and regards both men and women. What the Qur'ān recommends to both men and women is conduct of "decency" and "sobriety," both physical and moral. Concerning women, the general and subtle wording regarding "appearance" is proof of the great "flexibility" offered to them by the spiritual message to enable them to balance their spiritual beliefs and respective social contexts. The Qur'ān does nothing to legislate a "uniform" that would be strictly "Islamic," as some are trying to do at present. The first spiritual objective was not to lay down rigid rules regarding a "dress code" that would be fixed, once and for all, but rather to "recommend" an "attitude," or an "ethic," of both body and mind.

It is truly regrettable that the prime intention of the spiritual message is often left out, or completely ignored, sacrificed by a literal reading that limits any Qur'ānic teaching regarding women to the purported "obligation to wear the *hijāb*." This all goes against the principles of the universal message and its spiritual ethic. The question of the *khimār* or headscarf is part and parcel of the morals, behavior, and ethics of Islam. This falls within the area that Islamic science called *mu'āmalāt*, the social sphere or human relations, and not the domain of *'Ibādāt*, the practice of ritual. A religious conviction involving faith has meaning only when it is lived, without restraint. To speak of an Islamic obligation to wear a headscarf or a *khimār* cannot be spiritually acceptable because there too the Qur'ān is clear: "No compulsion in religion!" This is one of the fundamental principles of Islam.

Moreover, to reduce the comprehensive ethic of the Qur'ān about the body down to the theme of the "veil" is contrary to that same message. And this is exactly what has happened throughout Islamic history, as the force of focusing the entire Qur'ānic message on the single issue of the dress conduct of women, and the requirement that a woman must "hide" and "veil" her body, we in the Muslim world have "succeeded" in converting the spirituality of the message into a symbol of female oppression that is difficult to rectify.

For the Muslim women of today, the real challenge is to recover the liberating breath of the spiritual message of Islam. Wearing a headscarf is not, in itself, a spiritual target. Those who do not "feel" the need to do so have the freedom to live their spirituality outside of this standard "garment." And those who feel a need to follow this prescription and see it as a profound experience of intimacy and inwardness with the Creator also have the freedom to live their spirituality within the "garment" standard. In both cases, it is a matter of living one's spirituality according to the same liberating approach. The headscarf is a part of the ethic and is, before all, a woman's right. Women must have the right to choose to wear it or not to wear it, knowingly (an informed decision), because the right to wear it is inevitably linked to the right not to wear it. It should also attempt to overcome the binary vision that has always accompanied this theme and stop the headscarf from being used as an evaluation criterion of Muslim women. According to the ideological vision to which we adhere, some see it as a criterion of oppression, with those not wearing it inevitably judged as emancipated, while for others it is an indicator of the degree of faith, and that not to wear it is symptomatic of a lack of conviction or a weakness of faith. Now, one can never repeat it often enough, faith is not measured through the criteria of appearance, and we cannot afford to make value judgments about people based on their clothing behavior.

It is therefore clear that the main purpose of the Qur'ān is to encourage men and women to free themselves from all materialistic alienations and from seduction codes, peculiar to each era, and that are ultimately concrete projections of dominant ideologies recurring through the history of human civilization.

The Qur'ān invites men and women to appropriate a culture of decency and mutual respect: "But the raiment of reverence [*libās at-taqwā*], that is better. This is among the signs of God, that haply they may remember" (7:26). This verse, on its own, summarizes the central message that should be remembered and put into practice, in the present great chaos of ultra-liberal consumption, exuberance, arrogance, and the cult of appearance, as if they are Islamic ethics. What we are short of today is *libās at-taqwā*, the garment of the internality, which is inevitably reflected in the externality of the deeds and the actions of every man and every woman; it is this ethic of interiority, the moral rigor and decency that is preferable in the eyes of the Creator.

CHAPTER 15

The Equality of In-Court Testimony

One of the pejorative assertions against Islam concerns the claim that, in the Qur'ān, the testimony of a woman is valued at one-half of that of a man. According to this simplistic view, standing alone, this rule summarizes Islam's alleged disparaging view of women and confirms the privilege accorded to men, at the expense of women, whose intrinsic value would accordingly be equivalent to half of men's. In fact, this concept is expressed by both Islamophobic opponents and some Muslim ideologues who favor a patriarchal reading of the Qur'ānic text and defend what seems "self-evident" in their eyes with great conviction and sometimes naive sincerity.

The alleged general rule, extracted from a single verse, related to a particular situation, is actually contradicted by other Qur'ānic verses that very clearly establish the equality between women and men in matters of testimony. But by the simple force of being diffused and transmitted from generation to generation, this abusive assertion of unequal testimony has overshadowed the profound egalitarian meaning that we see in other verses that outline the core principles of testimony and are far more significant than the single verse that cites the summons of a man and two women.

In fact, we are herein before an instance of the type of information that has been pulled away from its general framework by commentators' reductive and literalist readings. By doing so, they have completely disregarded the mention of any of the other verses and focused on the one that is "apparently" more consistent with the dominant culture

© The Author(s) 2018   165
A. Lamrabet, *Women and Men in the Qur'ān*,
https://doi.org/10.1007/978-3-319-78741-1_15

of inequality between men and women. We note that, even today, some Muslim scholars expend their energy trying to justify the alleged principle of inequality in testimony and attribute it to the extreme "sensitivity" of women and their "fragile" memory, especially during periods of hormonal imbalance. Some even base their arguments on pseudoscientific theories that "confirm" the recurrent psychological instability of women and thus "scientifically" justify their vision of structural inequality between men and women.

THE TESTIMONY OF A MAN AND TWO WOMEN

Every time one ventures to assert gender equality in the name of Islamic principles, it is the verse about the "testimony of a man and two women" that is systematically cited, giving the impression that the verse, on its own, encapsulates the entire Qur'ānic vision on the matter:

> O you who believe! When you contract a debt with one another for a term appointed, write it down. And let a scribe write between you justly, and let not any scribe refuse to write as God taught him [*istashhidū*]. So let him write, and let the debtor dictate, and let him reverence God his Lord, and diminish nothing from it. And if the debtor is feeble-minded or is weak, or is unable to dictate himself, then let his guardian dictate justly. And call to witness two witnesses from among your men, and if there are not two men, then a man and two women from among those whom you approve as witnesses, so that if one of the two errs, the other can remind her.[1]

First, we should note that, strictly speaking, this verse speaks about an "attestation" (*ishhād*) rather than a "testimony" (*shahāda*).[2] In short, the verse is concerned with the attestation established between a creditor and a borrower, hence a matter of financial liability.

Most commentaries agree that the verse falls under the rubric of guidelines or recommendations (*irshād*) and not, strictly speaking, legislation (*tashrī'*). It is addressed to creditors to instruct them on a certain

---

[1] The Qur'ān 2:282.

[2] For more precision, see the work of the Egyptian scholar Muhammad 'Imārra, *At-tahrīr al-islāmī lil-mar'a* (Dār ash-shurūq, 2002), p. 82. Also see the argument of Sheikh 'Alī Jumu'a (Gomaa), the Mufti of Egypt, who confirms that verse 282 of *sūrah* 2 speaks about attestation (*ishhād*) and not testimony (*shahāda*) in *Almar'a fī al-hadāra al-islāmiyya* (Dār As-salām, 2008), p. 44.

issue or to recommend a course of action pertaining to a financial transaction between two parties—an "attestation" in due form as a precau-
tionary measure to protect the rights of creditors. This is exactly why
many Muslim jurists determined that since the verse concerns a specific
case—a financial transaction between two individuals—it cannot be used
as a source of legislation.[3] Ibn Taymiyya affirms that the verse calls on
two women when there is only one man present to attest, due to the
fact that, in general, women at the time were not accustomed to dealing
with financial transactions of this sort. He specifies, however, that if the
women were to acquire the skill and experience appropriate for the subject matter, then without any doubt their testimonies would be equal to
that of men.[4]

It is interesting how some Muslim scholars, knowing well that the
verse was revealed as a recommendation, continue to hold unto the
reductionist notion of the equivalence of two women to one man, and
continue to cite the verse, not in reference to the attestation recommendation in cases of financial debts, but in order to justify the inferiority of
women in all cases of testimony, irrespective of the situation.

The objective of this Qur'ānic verse was the establishment of an ethic
of conduct regarding enforcement clauses in contracts between people concluding a deed of financial services to ensure the protection of
right-holders. The provisions and means to implement this kind of attestation are established according to the conventions and social environment of each era. In the era of the Qur'ānic revelation, like many other
societies at that time, the operations of commercial affairs were dominated by men. Despite the fact that women had been kept distant from
such matters, the Qur'ān advocated their participation and presence in
such situations, as appropriate.[5]

Thus, this verse offers yet another important example of the progressive approach taken by the Qur'ān for the establishment of reforms in
favor of the integration of women in all social activities. Accordingly,
through this example of commercial transactions, the Qur'ān has opened
the door to the Muslim women of the era to participate, in a modest
way at first, in a tightly closed world of business, by bringing them in as

---

[3] These include some early jurists such as Ibn Taymiyya and his disciple Ibn Qayyim and
some contemporary ones such as Muhammad 'Abduh and Muhammad Shaltūt.

[4] Cf. Ibn Qāyyim al-Jawziyya, *I'lām al-muwaqqi'īn*, vol. 1, p. 95.

[5] Cf. Tāhā Jābir al-Alwānī, *The Testimony of Women in Islamic Law*.

attesters, to start with, no matter that it was initially done by calling on the attestation of two women as matching that of one man, given women's inexperience in the field.

EQUAL TESTIMONY IN THE TRANSMISSION OF THE SPIRITUAL MESSAGE

In several verses, the Qur'ān calls on men and women believers as equal members of the same community of faith to testify before the rest of humanity:

> Thus did We make you a middle community [*wasat*], that you may be witnesses [*shuhadās*] for mankind and that the Messenger may be a witness for you.[6]
>
> And strive for God as He should be striven for. He has chosen [for] you — and has placed no hardship for you in the religion — the creed of your father Abraham. He named you Muslims aforetime, and herein, that the Messenger may be a witness for you, and that you may be witnesses [*shuhadā'*] for mankind. So perform the prayer and give the alms, and hold fast to God. He is your Master. How excellent a Master, and how excellent a Helper![7]

In these verses, the Qur'ān speaks of a community of faith, the shared faith of men and women believers, one of the particularities of which is being a community of the "middle ground" or the "right balance" (*wasat*). According to most commentators, this qualifier, *wasat*, corresponds to the value of justice. The Prophet himself described *al-wasat* (the middle ground) as the "demand for justice" (*al-'adl*).[8]

This community is composed of women and men who are, according to the verse, the witnesses (*shuhadā'*) of a spiritual message whose first vocation is that of the execution of justice and respect of law. These women and men must bear witness to justice in their everyday acts and to ensure that this requirement is reflected in their society and before all of humanity. This is what the Prophet has explained in a *hadīth*: "The angels are God's witnesses in the heavens, and you are God's witnesses

---

[6] The Qur'ān 2:143.
[7] Ibid. 22:78.
[8] Cf. *Tafsīr Tabarī*.

on earth." And he followed up with the verse: "Say, 'Perform your deeds. God will see your deeds.'"⁹ Thus, being a witness, in this life, consists of being guided by a sense of equality and justice in all of one's actions; then God shall decide. According to the Qur'ān, witnessing (*shahāda*) is intimately related to the assertion of justice. To be able to act as a witness, in this sense, one should be just and have the moral consciousness of eternal fairness, no matter the circumstances.

Another verse in the Qur'ān relates testimony to a state of being equitable: "and call two just persons among yourselves to witness and uphold the testimony for God."¹⁰ Another *hadīth* expresses the same idea: "Only the righteous will testify." The commentator Al-Rāzī specifies that the verse addresses all believers, those who were present at the moment of the Revelation and those who came after, until eternity. He also reminds us that God has imposed the demand for justice as a condition for being a witness and that believers will bear witness via their fair acts in this world and in the hereafter.¹¹

The witnessing cited in these two verses thus concerns men and women who will bear witness through their acts in favor of justice and the rule of law, before God and before humanity in its entirety. Before all, such witnessing is the practice of faith for the service of humanity on earth. It thus reflects the spiritual commitment of each man and each woman in this world and the hereafter. Those who will be witnessing are those who will profoundly assimilate this message of justice and know how to apply it in their relationships with others. At every step of life, such witnessing shall try to awaken in the hearts of men and women believers their sense of responsibility toward others, toward the poorest, and to revive their empathy and sensitivity to other people's misery and the contingencies of earthly life. These verses summarize the entire Qur'ānic ethic in reference to bearing witness and constitute the normative framework within which one evaluates equality in the true sense of the word. Which equality could be more important than the one that allows men and women to bear witness before humanity and before their Creator?

⁹The Qur'ān 9:105; *hadīth* reported in the *Tafsīr* of Tabari, a commentary on the verse.

¹⁰Ibid., 65:2. In the context of a couple's wish to stay married at the end of the mandatory waiting period of three months, after the initiation of divorce procedures. In such a case, two witnesses must be called.

¹¹Al-Rāzī, *Mafātīh al-ghayb*.

Ibn Qayyim al-Jawziyya justifies legal equality of men and women in reference to witnessing via the previously cited Qur'ānic verse. In fact, the community of which the Qur'ān speaks is one that is composed of men and women, and there are no differences between the witnessing of the two components of humanity. The equality of witnessing, intended as a daily act of righteousness and moral commitment, provides the regulatory framework for evaluating each human being, man, or woman. Men and women, according to this Qur'ānic vision, are completely equal in terms of the greatest of testimonies, the testimony of heart and noble deeds. The Creator has not in the least differentiated between men and women in terms of bearing witness for justice on earth; the best among you will be he or she who meets the criterion of "noble ethics" (makārim al-akhlāq).

THE EQUALITY OF TESTIMONY IN THE CASE OF ADULTERY

In Islam, as in all other monotheistic traditions but also in conformance with all universal moral norms, adultery is solemnly condemned. The Qur'ān firmly forbids adultery in the following terms: "As for the adulterer and the adulteress, flog them each one hundred lashes."[12] It should be noted at the outset that, as punishment for proven adultery, the Qur'ān does not stipulate stoning, as some would like us to believe, but "a hundred lashes" that, as we shall see, would serve as a deterrent sanction. It is also very important to note that the Qur'ānic prescription concerning adultery addresses, all at once, men and women, contrary to the popular belief that only women will be incriminated and be held responsible in the case of adultery.

Before all, it is necessary to clear a common misconception around the stoning of adulterous women in Islam, a topic that continues to cause much ink to flow, with some asserting that this "practice" speaks volumes about the "barbarism" of Islam. Let us say it from the start and without deviation: There are no verses in the Qur'ān that speak of stoning women or men. The Qur'ānic punishment prescribed for adultery, both men and women, is flagellation (flogging, whipping)—the Qur'ān speaks of "one hundred lashes"—which was intended as a measure to repeal and replace the practice of stoning until death, which was a

[12]The Qur'ān 24:2.

common practice among Jewish and Arab communities of Medina at the time of the Prophet.

Unfortunately, the practice of stoning has long survived in Arabia, resisting all attempts at reform, despite the total absence of such a punishment in the Qur'ān. Islamic law (*Fiqh*), on the other hand, will maintain the concept of stoning, so that subsequent practice is justified on the basis of a controversial interpretation of some *hadīths* concerning a few cases of adultery that were voluntarily admitted by the guilty parties during the Medina period.

We should specify here that the Qur'ān has deliberately repealed the practice of stoning and replaced it by the corporal punishment of one hundred lashes, a penalty that aimed to be dissuasive as, at the time, stoning was reflected in the penal system that was recognized just about everywhere. The human civilizations of the era, no matter the religious persuasion, had but this type of corporal punishment, stoning, which formed a part of the law enforcement penalties of the era.

It is important to point out, however, that, in connection with the first adultery cases accusing women, the Qur'ān, in a first phase, issued a binding measure to "detain" women accused of adultery in their homes until further notice:

> As for those of your women who commit an indecency, call four witnesses among you to bear witness against them. And if they bear witness, then confine them to their houses until death takes them or until God appoints for them another way.[13]

The first thing that comes to one's attention in this verse is that the Qur'ān requires, before all, the testimony of four people who have witnessed the act, almost impossible to realize. "Confining" women who have been accused of adultery in their homes might be considered a way of protecting these women who could, otherwise, become victims of popular stigma and disgrace. The confinement was also an interim solution to prevent the application of the law of stoning, which was still in force.[14]

---

[13] The Qur'ān 4:15.

[14] Cf. Dr. al-'Ajamī, "Adultère et lapidation," in *Que dit vraiment le Coran?* (SRBs Editions, 2008), p. 44.

This measure of "house arrest" would remain unapplied because, in the unanimous opinion of virtually all commentators, it was repealed by another Qur'ānic verse that defines the legal provisions related to adultery. In fact, the following verse marks the second step in the Qur'ānic reform regarding adultery:

> And as for those who accuse chaste women, but then do not bring four witnesses, flog them eighty lashes, and never accept any testimony from them. And it is they who are the iniquitous.[15]

The abolition of stoning—equivalent to a death sentence—by the Qur'ān, and its substitution by a corporal punishment represented in the one hundred lashes, was already a huge step forward toward easing the penalty; but what was more important is that the Qur'ān also required irrefutable evidence of adultery.

It is clear that this Qur'ānic measure of proven adultery renders incrimination exceptionally difficult, if not impossible. A proof of adultery requires the presence of four eyewitnesses who, according to Muslim law, must testify that they have seen it happen and that the versions of the four witnesses completely coincide, which is virtually impossible.[16]

The new measure thus remains extremely difficult to implement because it is conditioned by the concordance of the versions of the four eyewitnesses. The obligation to provide four eyewitnesses is a drastic condition that makes the confirmation of the adulterous act very improbable, especially because the Qur'ān is strict about the penalty of false testimony—the same punishment as adulterers, namely flogging (eighty lashes rather then the hundred for adulterers) and a loss of all civic rights.[17] Given that the legal principles regarding adultery were revealed gradually, a legal vacuum forced the Prophet to apply punitive

---

[15] The Qur'ān 24:4.

[16] It is surprising that Islamic law has preserved the rule of stoning while posing very demanding conditions as to proof of adultery, including specific details, e.g., the need to pass a wire between the bodies of the protagonists to prove it has actually happened. It is strictly contradictory to uphold stoning for adultery while formally affirming the impossibility of providing acceptable evidence.

[17] An unsubstantiated accusation is an offense called *qadhf* in the Qur'ān and is punishable by eighty lashes (24:4–9).

sanctions that were known at the time, under pressure from the population, including the erudite of the Jewish faith who strongly endorsed the stoning ordinance.

A large number of *hadīths* attest to the understanding and compassion with which the Prophet dealt with those who came to him to confess their "sins." At times, he tried to put what he was told into perspective; other times, he tried to extend the term or to pretend that he had not recorded the alleged facts in order to give those who came voluntarily to confess their crimes the opportunity to retract what they had revealed to him. In this respect, it is interesting to note that it was on the basis of the *hadīths* of the Prophet that Islamic law has developed the notion of "doubt" or "ambiguity" (*shubha*), which cancels, at any time, the adultery conviction.

The Qur'ān has thus tried to establish a very reformist vision in order to advance the social mores of the era by invalidating the Hebrew law of stoning on the one hand and teaching Muslims to respect the private lives of people on the other. Besides, after the Revelation of the second verse that stipulated the presence of witnesses, some of the Prophet's Medina companions have openly expressed their disapproval of measures that the mindset of the era was not yet ready to understand, let alone embrace. In fact, Ibn Kathīr reports that at the announcement of verse 24 of *sūrah* 4, many of the Prophet's companions were outraged that, faced with such an offensive crime, it was necessary to have four witnesses in order to prosecute the perpetrators.

One can understand the dismay of the Arabs of the era, proud and firmly attached to honor and social reputation and used to resolving such conflicts through the personal settling of scores.[18] And this was exactly the question that one of the companions of the Prophet went to talk to him about: "How can a man behave if he finds another man with his wife: should he not kill him?"[19] The Muslims of the era started wondering what they could do in the absence of eyewitnesses if a man captured his wife with another man, in *flagrante delicto* (red-handed), but he was the only eyewitness. According to most commentators, it was in the aftermath of a series of such outbursts that the following verse was revealed:

---

[18] Cf. *Tafsīr Ibn Kathīr*. Various *hadīths* on this subject were reported by Ahmad.
[19] Cf. supra.

And as for those who accuse chaste women, but then do not bring four witnesses, flog them eighty lashes and never accept any testimony from them. And it is they who are iniquitous, save those who repent thereafter and make amends, for truly God is Forgiving, Merciful. And as for those who accuse their wives and have no witnesses but themselves, then the testimony of one of them shall be four testimonies, swearing by God that he is among the truthful, and the fifth shall be that the curse of God be upon him if he is among the liars. And the punishment shall be averted from her should she give four testimonies, swearing by God that he is among the liars, and the fifth that God's Wrath shall come upon her, if he is among the truthful.[20]

Thus, in the case where someone, man or woman, accuses his or her spouse of adultery but is unable to produce four eye witnesses, the Qur'ān allows the matter to be decided by the pledging of oaths—swearing four consecutive times, before God and in front of a judge, to the accuracy of the accusation. And there will be a fifth oath, called *li'ān*, in Islamic law, that invokes a divine curse upon the one swearing if not telling the truth. The person accused can do exactly the same thing in his or her defense. Clearly, if each performs the pledge of oaths, including the *li'ān*, there will be no proof of the culpability of either partner, accuser, or defendant, because it is assumed to be an oath made in good faith and sincerity by both, but neither can provide any material proof, one way or another.

Again, let us take note of what the Qur'ān requires with respect to this extremely sensitive issue of adultery and observe the language employed by the sacred text, which aims at dissuading believers from succumbing to the temptation that will unquestionably be deeply damaging to the moral integrity of the persons involved, on both sides: the pain and injury caused by the betrayal of the intimacy of hearts and bodies.

This verbal confrontation of *li'ān* between the husband and wife symbolizes an egalitarian exchange of evidence, done via the two equal testimonies, with each person's own conscience being the only judge. The brilliant jurist Ibn Rushd affirms that this verse of *li'ān* expresses the concept of testimony in the truest sense of the word because it is conditioned by the same criteria as the common testimony and because it is

---

[20]The Qur'ān 24:4–9.

for all who can testify. In this, Ibn Rushd relies on the following passage of the verse: "then the testimony of one of them shall be four testimonies, swearing by God that he is among the truthful."

We are here confronted with one of the most striking examples of the equality in testimony of a man and a woman, which touches the most valuable dimension of the intimate life of a couple, namely the bonds of loyalty and mutual trust. This testimony is very important because it concerns the covenant sealing the moral commitment that establishes the deep bond between a man a woman, before God and Man.

How can one continue to speak of unequal testimony even though we have here an example of the incontestable equality between a man and a woman, and in an area that touches one of the most tragic situations that a couple could go through and which can put an end to the future of an entire family? The Qur'ān, more than fourteen centuries ago, legislated in a manner difficult to surpass, including by modern standards, on an issue as controversial as adultery—it does not recommend anything less than a reciprocal exchange of witnesses and testimony of faith between husband and wife before a judge.

It is important to keep in mind that, once this solemn confrontation terminates, the judge, according to the majority of Islamic jurisprudence schools, finds himself obligated to pronounce an immediate divorce because the basic trust that legitimizes a marital union has been ruptured beyond repair by the reciprocal accusations of adultery.[21]

One cannot but marvel at the huge contrast we see between the pacifist, reasoned, and pioneering posture of the Qur'ān on the one hand and the laws in force in some Muslim countries since the colonial period on the other, laws that hardly reflect the importance that this Qur'ānic concept deserves to the extent that, in some countries, legislation in favor of what amounts to "honor killings" remains the norm. Thus, men are given the right to kill women alleged to having breached the code of family honor, since, in their minds, only women are guardians of the family honor, and legitimizing such horrible crimes in the name of Islam. We should recognize, however, that the practice of honor killings is not the prerogative of Muslim societies alone—far from it. It is a custom that is practiced, to varying degrees, by many societies, no matter the sociocultural milieu. One has only to see how, in European laws, the former

---

[21] See the discussion and differences concerning the modalities of divorce in the legal treatise of Ibn Rushd (supra).

honor killings have been replaced, with the modernization of laws and morals, by the more watered-down concept of "crimes of passion."[22]

Thus, and without any hesitation, we can confirm that the Qur'ān was very pioneering in its approach to the problem of adultery and that the solutions recommended by the sacred text have allowed the resolution of the conflict serenely, outside of any compulsive action. Thus, the example of equal testimony in the case of adultery, on its own, testifies to the egalitarian approach of the Qur'ān and repudiates irrefutably the incorrect charges concerning the inequality of testimony in Islam.

Finally, let us not overlook the legal principle in Islam that stipulates that a man and a woman are equal in their ability to transmit a *hadīth*. No doubt, the transmission of a *hadīth* is on par with testimony. If that is indeed the case, how can one affirm that the testimony of women is accepted relative to the sayings and doings of the Prophet but rejected when it concerns someone else? One is, however, entitled to raise a number of questions concerning the existing discrepancy between what is in the Qur'ān and the reality of Muslims. Given the ease with which one may find, with precision, the needed information in the Qur'ān, how is it that Muslims continue to justify the unequal testimony when the Qur'ān clearly asserts the equality of testimony of men and women, and to uphold and excuse stoning in the case of adultery when stoning is simply not mentioned in the Qur'ānic texts and (1) the evidence of adultery is very difficult to satisfy and (2) the penalty for adultery applies equality to both men and women?

Now is perhaps the time to go back to our scriptural sources for responses to all of these questions and to stop endorsing inequality in the name of Islamic principles. The question of the equality of testimony should not even be raised because the Qur'ān has responded to it centuries before the appearance of modern legislations.

---

[22] In France, the legal disposition relative to honor crimes has disappeared from law texts with the reform of the criminal law of 1791 and was tacitly replaced by "crime of passion" where, half the time, the criminal responsible for the murder of the wife accused of adultery was acquitted.

PART III

Equality, the Time of a Revelation

CHAPTER 16

Why Is There a Lag?

Having highlighted the objectives of the Qur'ānic egalitarian ethic and principles that underlie and govern the relations between men and women in Islam, it becomes clearly evident that such ethic is virtually absent in contemporary Muslim thought, in the reality of Muslim lives, and in their conception or practice of religion. Beyond a shadow of doubt, there exists a significant lag between the egalitarian vision of the Qur'ān and the manner in which Islam is experienced. And there are a number of inherent reasons behind this perception of gender inequality.

Conducting an in-depth analysis of this question—the strong perception of inequality in Islam—has not been the primary objective of this book. We can nevertheless identify, in a summary fashion, the most probable reasons behind the persistent continuation of the lag between Qur'ānic norms and Islamic social norms by organizing them into three categories: sociocultural, political, and legal.

As would be expected, the sociocultural dimension is very well established, since in Islam—as indeed is the case with all other religions—the weight of customs, history, and the earlier interpretations of the founding texts, not to mention the underlying cultural norms, have served to uphold a certain religious vision of gender inequality. This inequality is also rooted in the universal culture of human civilization, of which no society was or is exempt. Despite all of that, some societies are more marked by this than others, to the extent that they have a certain sociocultural predisposition, as is indeed the case of the Arabian Peninsula, deeply entrenched in an ancient patriarchal tribal tradition. By virtue of

© The Author(s) 2018
A. Lamrabet, *Women and Men in the Qur'ān*,
https://doi.org/10.1007/978-3-319-78741-1_16

its religious and normative centrality, this region, the sacred home of the Islamic Revelation and the "Mecca" of the production of Islamic sciences, has strongly contributed to the perpetuation of cultural relations of domination, inequality, and discrimination against women and, from there, to the generalization of these attributes through a dogmatic and standardized reading of the Sacred Text.

Thus, the last monotheist religion was grafted on a cultural system that was shaped by patriarchy, a culture of booty, and slavery, all of which formed an integral part of the society and were even considered part and parcel of the "natural order." For centuries, this state of affairs has significantly contributed to impeding the application of the egalitarian standards of the spiritual message of Islam; one might even say that it proved to be a real barrier to all rational readings of the scriptural sources—the Qur'ān and the traditions (sayings and doings) of the Prophet.

As a result, the balanced and harmonious relationship between men and women, as preached by the Qur'ān and embodied in the enlightening example of the Prophet, was read, understood, and interpreted in accordance with the powerful cultural triad of patriarchy, booty, and slavery. In short, the impact of the ancestral customs and socioeconomic understandings of their period of history on the readings and interpretations of the Sacred Text resulted in muddying the issues at hand and distorting the egalitarian norms of the Qur'ān and the *hadīth*.

Thus, the early scholars projected their personal aspirations, their ideas, their conception of social order and norms, and their deeply rooted prejudices in the elaboration of what is thought of as "Islamic law" (*Fiqh*) but which, deep down, was very far from Qur'ānic ideals, having done no more than reflect the normative values of the era. Today, the fact that the early scholars were highly influenced by their sociocultural environment is not the root cause of the problem. Men have always legislated in reference to a given social framework, taking into account their value system and drawing on their respective sociocultural contexts. The real problem we are facing today lies in the general inability and unwillingness of contemporary scholarship to recognize and to take into account the evolution of time and social mutations over the last few centuries, thereby maintaining laws that have become, by definition, obsolete.

This is what has taken place in the different Muslim societies where the laws that were produced by the early schools of Islamic jurisprudence became irreversible and valid for all times, even sacred, as if they were decreed by the Qur'ān itself. Thus, instead of going back to the original sources and doing a series job of rereading the Sacred Text, subsequent generations of scholars, in their great majority, almost always behaved as if they were compelled to revert back to the opinions of the early scholars, in total disregard of their own realities, their experiences, and their respective contexts.

It would be useful to keep in mind here that the "sacredness" of the earlier legal statutes was solidified and established in the Muslim world at the beginning of the decline of the Muslim civilization; whether this was carried out by fear, by weakness, or by an identitarian closure,[1] they seem to have decided to hide behind the walls of social immobility and intellectual sclerosis in the illusory hope of better protection. It is interesting to note, in this regard, that the early Muslim scholars, particularly the founders of Islamic jurisprudence schools, never stated or assumed that their knowledge and their interpretations of the sources were on the order of the sacred and should remain immutable. In this respect, the example of Mālik ibn Anas, the founder of the Māliki School is revealing. The second Abbasid Caliph al-Mansūr (714–775) asked Mālik to write a legal abstract in which he should "avoid the radicalism of Ibn 'Umar and the permissiveness of Ibn Abbās," both of whom were eminent scholars of the first hour of Islam. When this law treatise was completed—called al-Muwatta' by Mālik—al-Mansūr wanted to impose Mālik's codification on the entire Islamic Empire. Mālik rejected the idea categorically, responding: "Allow the people to choose the rules that better correspond to the context of where they live."[2]

On the other hand, it is important to underscore that, despite the fact that the patriarchal sociocultural realities have, for a long time, marked in an obvious manner the subsequent readings and interpretations of the Sacred Text, some fundamental egalitarian ideas of the Qur'ān, still infused with the original spiritual ethic, managed to survive, due to the insight of some scholars of early generations, whose thorough knowledge of the text allowed them to play this important role. This is the case, among others, of the financial autonomy of Muslim women, which has been systematically recognized by the different Islamic law doctrines,

---

[1] An emphasis on ethnic and cultural homogeneity and a serious dislike of what might be viewed as Western liberalism and globalization.

[2] 'Ali Hasballah, *Usoul at-Tashrī' al-Islāmi* (Idarah Al-Qur'ān, 1987), p. 85. Also cited by 'Alī Jumua', *Taghyīr al-fatwā bi taghyīr az-zmān wa al-makān*.

over fourteen centuries ago.[3] The appointment of a woman to the post of "financial controller" (*muhtasib*) under the caliphate of 'Umar ibn-al-Khattāb is a very well-known example. The social role of the *hisba* (calculation) as a market and commerce controller was a very important post because it concerned transposing a cohesive and equitable economic ethic at the level of the society.

The fact that a woman would be appointed to such a post, especially at that time—approximately fourteen centuries ago—reflects the influence of the egalitarian spirit of the spiritual message that the early companions knew how to preserve despite their cultural heritage. Unfortunately, we must admit that this type of example, while very impressive for the era, remains a rarity in the course of Islamic history; the heavy cultural heritage will take over the few enlightened minds that cannot fight against tribal customs, still too ingrained in social mores. Thus, the patriarchal cultural component has constituted a real obstacle to the diffusion and rise of the egalitarian message of Islam; needless to say, it was also assisted by the political crisis of the early years of Islam that resulted in the marginalization of the entire liberating process of Islam for women as well as men.

In fact, the turmoil and political fractures that Muslims experienced after the death of the Prophet, during the period known as "the great discord" (*fitna*), contributed to the closure of the spiritual message of Islam and the obfuscation of its values of justice, liberty, and social equality while encouraging subservience and fatalism.

The political dimension has thus played a prominent role in shaping the orientation of all subsequent Islamic intellectual productivity. In fact, the compilation of Islamic law has coincided with the establishment of political despotism and autocracy in the land of Islam, especially with the advent of hereditary monarchy, which was inaugurated by Mu'āwiyah.[4]

This situation has inevitably engendered the marginalization of fundamental societal issues such as liberty and justice in favor of a generated cycle of legal documents that are focused exclusively on matters of personal status, morality, and cultural practice and norms. Thus, with the establishment of a political culture of submission and a genuine ideology of blind obedience to government, a large proportion of Islamic

[3] In comparison, in England, this right was not granted to women until 1882.

[4] Mu'āwiyah ibn Abī Sufyān (602–680) was the founder of the Umayyad Dynasty after fighting with the fourth *Rashidūn* Caliph, 'Ali, the Prophet's cousin and son-in-law.

sciences were limited only to cultural and personal dimensions, as well as structural interpretations of text (grammar, rhetoric, etc.), without any correlation with the rest of the socioeconomic and political environment.

On the legal side, the "*Fiqh* of submission" has thus rigidly focused on ritualism and the codification of customary laws, leaving out the aims of the Qur'ānic message, its universal ethics, rights, liberties, and the principles of equality as they were proclaimed in the Qur'ān and in the *Sunnah* (the sayings and doings of the Prophet). The laws produced under political despotism will thus become responsible for the hypertrophy of legal *Fiqh* at the expense of other records—spiritual, philosophical, and ethical. The *Fiqh* will thus spread exclusively within its legal dimension, giving over time the image of an Islam that has been strictly reduced to the normative, improperly identified by some as *Sharī'a*, the divine law itself. Interestingly, *Sharī'a* and *Fiqh* are parts of two distinct registers, and the confusion between the two is the source of all the interpretative extremes.

It is important to recognize *Sharī'a* as a Qur'ānic concept that describes a path, a model, and a global system that includes ethics, morality, divine orientations, and universal principles. *Sharī'a* is not a code of laws but a way, or rather the way, that leads to a Qur'ānic ideal and guides men and women believers in their spiritual journey. The *Fiqh*, on the other hand, as the name indicates, signifies "comprehension." The *faqīh* is an erudite, one who engages in the research for knowledge and the comprehension of religious information and prescriptions, starting with the Sacred Written Book (*al-kitāb al-mastūr*) along with the Book of Creation (*al-kitāb al-manshūr*).

As much as the *Sharī'a*, in its ideal form, is a concept that remains divine and corresponds with the search for perfection and spiritual excellence, so much would the comprehension of such ideal not be anything but the fruit of a human intellectual effort, and hence imperfect. The *Sharī'a* is a divine inspiration and stays imperceptible in its infinity; its comprehension, however, must remain humanly possible and translatable in terms of the realities of all believers. It is, then, this comprehension of the *Sharī'a* that connects the eternal spiritual dimension in its universal purposes to the cyclical reality of our experiences, which is inevitably in perpetual motion.

Nevertheless, as of the second century of *Hijra*,[5] the *Fiqh* is distanced from its primary calling of comprehension and contextualization of sources and is progressively reduced to an essentialist legal conception. The countless subsequent compilations of *Fiqh* will forge a system of rules of legal treaties that will become increasingly codified and, via a semantic but also conceptual shift, will eventually displace the *Sharī'a* or even become confounded with its sacred dimension. It is important to note that *Fiqh* is not, never was, and never shall be a divine right because it only represents human understanding of the *Sharī'a*. In other words, it is a science that was advanced by scholars as they tried to adapt social legislation to the norms and sociopolitical environment of their eras, which are always in transformation. Thus, it is an ongoing process of *ijtihād*[6] to enable juridical norms to remain relevant to existing contexts of social standards. In this sense, *Fiqh* is a social construct that is in perpetual evolution, as it applies the laws of *Sharī'a*—the Qur'ānic guidance that, in terms of purpose, remains eternally universal—to our daily lives.

In its primary vocation, *Fiqh* is the "instrument" that should help men and women believers to maintain an active conscience and remain intelligent and attentive to their surroundings. Unfortunately, *Fiqh* got stuck in the technical codification of laws and rules, increasingly detailed and further removed, as a result of a narrow formalism of the compassionate realism and humanism of the Qur'ānic message.

We have witnessed how the different key concepts of equality have been interpreted by the *Fiqh* but also by classic commentaries in a way that transforms the Qur'ānic principles of marriage into rigid customary codes in which the subjugation of women is in order and the abusive male authority is an irrefutable legal norm. Marriage, which is a genuine pact between two partners, equal before God, was interpreted as if it were a sales contract where the entire legal structure revolves around the bodies of women and their possible subversion into eternal sources of detrimental temptation. Unfortunately, these notions remain very common, both in the academic curriculum of Islamic universities and in the religious discourse of some contemporary Muslim scholars.

---

[5] The "*hijra*" refers to the migration or journey of the Prophet and his followers from Mecca to Yathrib, which the Prophet renamed Medina in the year 622.

[6] Decisions and conclusions made by erudite individuals based on independent interpretations of the original sources of the Qur'ān and the *Sunnah*.

CHAPTER 17

What Alternative Possibilities?

To both impede and remedy the automatic transmission of discriminatory religious interpretations between and within generations, the first option to consider should be the initiation of a program of profound reform of Islamic teaching. In fact, a serious reform in religious fields cannot be undertaken without having carried out, first and foremost, a meaningful reform of the content of the teaching of Islamic sciences, including history, Islamic thought, exegeses (*tafāsīr* or commentaries), studies of the *hadīth*, and Islamic law (*Fiqh*). Islamic sciences should be reviewed and reevaluated from the perspective of both substance and form.

As currently carried out, Islamic teaching is based largely on the passive transmission of historical compilations. This must be replaced by a teaching philosophy and method that uses the tools and resources of modern education, including the historical approach and analytical tools of human and social sciences, for the study of scriptural texts and sources. And we urgently need to return to the employment of *ijtihād* as not only a concept and indispensable means of contextualizing scriptural sources but also in the conduct of critical analysis and synthesis, both of which are virtually absent in current Islamic teaching.

In the reassessment of the Islamic intellectual heritage, such reform should introduce or reintroduce the study of philosophy, sociology, anthropology, and modern legal sciences. It should also give importance to the study of the great philosophers and thinkers, including Sufi and Muslim philosophers of the golden age of Islam, and to teach Muslim

© The Author(s) 2018
A. Lamrabet, *Women and Men in the Qur'ān*,
https://doi.org/10.1007/978-3-319-78741-1_17

students the infinite value of openness and tolerance that are unique to the spiritual message of Islam.

And all reforms of Islamic law should be done in terms of the social and legal realities of the present time and contexts, as we simply cannot continue to apply the legal solutions that had been developed in the eighth century to problems we are facing in the twenty-first century. We are in desperate need of a *Fiqh* that can enlighten the minds and reasoning processes of Muslims, a *Fiqh* that is realistic, intelligent, coherent, and critical. The high councils of *'ulamā* should stop being the "fortresses" they are now, closed to the rest of Muslims. The *'ulamā*—men and women—can be specialists in Islamic sciences as well as other areas of knowledge, such as the humanities, social sciences, economics, and other specialties. These high councils must, therefore, be interdisciplinary because being a specialist in Islamic texts does not mean that they also have the required expertise in all other areas that affect and concern Muslims societies and the challenges and transformations that they face.

To be credible and able to protect the thoughts and ideas developed in the different projects, the specialists in the social, political, economic, and hard sciences must become an integral part of all high councils, must include men and women, and must be absolutely independent of the political power. And these high councils of *'ulamā* must become the democratic spaces in which members are freely able to discuss all contemporary issues, thereby establishing a culture of dialogue with all components of the society and in all areas of knowledge in order to free the minds of the current schizophrenic dichotomy of lawful versus unlawful (*Harām* vs. *Halāl*) of the current Islamic discourse.

It will also be critical to include and insist on gender equality as a requirement of religious reforms. In fact, a religious reform cannot be concretely achieved without such equality, inscribed in the heart of Islamic thought. For this, there should be a critical review of all discriminatory and sexist interpretations contained in the classical Islamic educational textbooks and which convey disparaging stereotypes about women.

CHAPTER 18

Equality, the Time of a Revelation

The conclusion is therefore clear. Apart from the early days of the Revelation, the egalitarian spirit of the Qur'ān and the tradition of the Prophet were almost never realized on the ground of reality, in the lives of Muslims, and throughout the history of Islamic civilization. Equality remained confined in the sacred text of the Qur'ān and the example of the Prophet. It was claimed, in theory, but it was never concretized. At a minimum, we need to recognize and admit this fact. And therein lies the problem of a value system that could never bring itself to reach the interpretations and the conclusions necessary to implement this egalitarian ethic.

Today, despite the resurgence—for several decades now—of a spiritual renaissance and the swelling waves of successive reformers who swept across the Muslim world demanding reform, revival, and *ijtihād*, it has not yet resulted in the emergence of a true fundamental reform of Islamic sciences, of *Fiqh*, or of Islamic thought. At the end, these valiant efforts have brought about only partial and superficial remedies for ailments that remain persistent and run deep.

The contributions of different contemporary "reformers" is rather weak because they are still a minority, remain extremely overcautious, and confine themselves to rationalization and defensive discourses rather than a profound reflection and effective contribution to current world realities.

In the Qur'ān, we have a major spiritual repository that is full of universal values such as equality, justice, generosity, awareness of the

© The Author(s) 2018
A. Lamrabet, *Women and Men in the Qur'ān*,
https://doi.org/10.1007/978-3-319-78741-1_18

Common Good, the requirement of empathy, and the love of good for the Other. But all of these values suffer as a result of not being formulated in a language and in an expression that matches our daily reality, or adapted to our experience. The return of "religiosity" is experienced as a return to the rigid formalism rather than a spirituality of commitment and a true consciousness of God. Yet, with the loss of meaning and values, our present world is much more in need of concrete actions rather than popular formalism and theoretical discourse. Our world today has more need for this ethical sense and morality to illuminate the bereaved perplexed hearts and wandering souls of our hypermodern lives. We are in desperate need of this spiritual awareness to calm our fears and weaknesses and advance serenely in helping each other. This is the equality that the Qur'ān speaks of, the equality of men and women who, together, live, help, and commit to each other, in confidence and exemplarity.

This is the equality that the Qur'ān speaks of: universal in its objectives of rights and obligations but formulated in reference to the particularities of a time and space. It is this equality that it is all about, one that ensures the dignity of every human being, one that no law, institution, or ideology has the right to take away.

It is this inner outlook of the Qur'ān, the word of God addressed to the hearts of people, that we need to learn to awaken and recapture, to hear once again in our inner selves, the most beautiful verses about equality, divine words that our hearts have been unable to recognize and appreciate, except at the very moment of Revelation.

REFERENCES

Abū Chouqqa, 'A. (1998). *Encyclopédie de la femme en Islam: la femme dans les textes du Saint Coran et des Ṣaḥīḥ d'al-Boukhārī et Mouslim*. France. Retrieved from http://catalog.hathitrust.org/Record/004046198.

Abū Nu'aym, Ahmad ibn 'Abd Allāh ibn Ahmad ibn Ishāq al-Asfahānī. *Faḍīlat al-'Ādilīna min al-wulāt as-salāṭīn* [Just governments and the duties of the governed towards the rulers].

Abū Shuqqa, 'A. (2011). *Taḥrīr al-mar'ah fī 'Aṣr al-risālah, dirāsah 'an al-mar'ah, jāmi'ah li-nuṣūṣ al-qur'ān al-karīm wa-ṣaḥīḥay al-bukhārī wa-mus-lim* (7th ed.). Kuwait: Dār al-Qalam lil-Nashr wa-al-Tawzī'.

Al-Baydāwi, Abd Allah Ibn 'Umar. (2013). In Fleischer, H. L. (Ed.), *Anwār al-tanzīl wa-asrār al-ta'wīl* (Bilingual ed.). Gorgias Pr Llc (Latin/Arabic).

Al-Bukhāri, I. M. *Sahih al-bukhari*, no. 273. Retrieved from https://sunnah.com/bukhari.

Al-Bukhāri, I. M. (2015). *Saḥīḥ al bukhāri*. Retrieved from https://sunnah.com/bukhari.

Al-Ghanushi, R. (2000). *Al-mar'a bayna al-qur'ān W wāqi' al-muslimīn*. London: The Maghreb Center for Research and Translation.

Al-Ghazāli, Abū Ḥāmid Muḥammad ibn Muḥammad. (1938). *Ihyā' 'ulūm ad-dīn* [The revival of religious sciences], 5 volumes. Cairo: Matba'ah Lajnah Nashr al-Thaqafah al-Islamiyyah.

Al-Hibri, A. Y. (2005). *Droits des femme musulmanes dans le village mondial: Défi et opportunités*. Retrieved from http://www.cfpe2004.fr/droits-des-femmes-musulmanes-dans-le-village-mondial-defis-et-opportunites-azizah-yahia-al-hibri.

Al-Jawzīyya, I. Q. (1973). *I'lām al-muwaqqi'īn 'an rabb al-'ālamīn.* Retrieved from http://data.theeuropeanlibrary.org/BibliographicResource/ 3000040691894.

Al-Jazīri, A. A. (2009). *Al-fiqh 'ala al-madhāhib al-arba'ah* [Islamic jurisprudence according to the four sunni schools]. Louisville, KY: Fons Vitae.

Al-Qaradhāwi, D. Y. (1998). *Min fiqh ad-dawla fi-l islām.* Cairo: Dār ash-Shurūq.

Al-Qushairī, M. I., & Tāmir, M. M. (2005). Sahīḥ muslim (aṭ-Ṭabʿa 1. ed.). al-Qāhira: Mu'assasat al-Muḥtār.

Al-Rāzi. (2005). Muhammad ibn Umar Fakhr al-Din. *Tafsīr al-rāzī, mafātīh al-ghayb, at-tafsīr al-kabīr* [Keys to the unknown]. Dar al-Fikr.

Al-Suyuti, Abū al-Faḍl 'Abd al-Raḥmān ibn Muḥammad Jalāl al-Dīn. *Al-jāmi' al-kabīr wal jāmi' as-saghīr.* www.muhaddith.org/hadith.html.

Al-Tabrisi, F. I. H. (1997). *Majmaʿ al-bayān fī tafsīr al-qurʾān* [Arabic] (al-Tab'ah 1 ed.). Beirut.

Al-Tirmīdhi, M. I. (1980). *Sunan al-tirmīdhi: Al-jamiul sahih* [Arabic]. Beirut: Darul Firkh.

Al-Wahīdi. (2006). *Asbāb an-nuzūl* [The reasons for the revelation]. Beirut: Dar Al-Kutub Al-'Ilmiya.

Alwani, T. J. (1996). The testimony of women in Islamic law. *American Journal of Islamic Social Sciences, 13*(2), 173. Retrieved from http://search.proquest.com/docview/1311898158.

Al-Wazīr, A. I. (2000). *Al-fardiyya* [Arabic]. Beirut: Al-Manāhil.

Al-Zamakhshari, Abū al-Qasim Mahmud ibn 'Umar. (1891). *Al-kashshāf 'an haqā'iq at-tanzīl* [The revealer] (1st ed.). Ann Arbor: University of Michigan Library.

An-Nīsābū, A. A. (2002). *Asbāb an-nuzūl* [The reasons for the revelation]. Beirut: Dār al-Jayl.

Ar-Rādi, S. A. (2009). *Nahj al-balāgha. A compilation of 'ali ibn tālib's sermons (241) letters (79), and 489 sayings (489)* (7th ed.). Tahrike Tarsile.

At-Tabari, I. J. *Tafsīr ibn jarīr at-tabarī - jami' aal-bayān 'an ta'wil al-qur'ān.* Riyad, Sa'udi: Dar 'Aalim al-Kutub.

At-Tabari, I. J. (1997). *Jāmiʿ al-bayān fī ta'wīl al-qurʾān* [The interpretation of the Qur'ān: A collection] (New ed.). Beirut: Dar al-Kutum al-'Ilmiya.

Attané, I. (2006). L'Asie manque de femmes. *Le Monde diplomatique.* Retrieved from http://www.cairn.info/article.php?ID_ARTICLE=news·20060701·MD·0003.

Bennabi, M. (2006). *Vocation de l'islam.* Beyrouth [u.a.]: Dar Albouraq [u.a.].

Buisset, A. (2008). *Les religions face aux femmes.* Paris: Ed. Accarias-l'Originel.

Courbage, Y., & Todd, E. (2007). *Le rendez-vous des civilisation, la république des idées.* France: Sueil.

Diagne, S. B. (2008). *Comment philosopher en islam?* Paris: Ed. du Panama.

Dr. Al-'Ajami. (2011). *Frapper sa femme avec le coran.* Retrieved from https://oumma.com/frapper-sa-femme-avec-le-coran-12/.

Dr. Al-'Ajami, A. N. (2008). *Que dit vraiment le coran.* France: Editeur.

El Hajjami, A. (2009). *Le code de la famille à l'épreuve de la pratique judiciaire.* Retrieved from http://www.sudoc.fr/162388721.

El-Fassi, A. (1973). *An-naqd adh-dhati* [Self-criticism]. Morocco: Erissala.

Encyclopedia of Women & Islamic Cultures. (2003). Netherlands. Retrieved from http://catalog.hathitrust.org/Record/004331195.

Exodus. (2001). Crossway Bibles, a publishing ministry of Good News Publishers.

Fruchtenbaum, A. G. (2009). *The book of genesis* (1st ed., J. Prinjinski, Ed.). Ariel Ministries.

Gauthier, D. P. (2006). *Rousseau: The sentiment of existence* (1 publ. ed.). Cambridge [u.a.]: Cambridge University Press.

Genesis 1. (2011). The Vatican: Libreria Editrice Vaticana.

Genesis 2. (2011). The Vatican: Libreria Editrice Vaticana.

Geoffroy, E. (2009). *L'islam sera spirituel ou ne sera plus.* Paris: Seuil.

Grajevsky, A. L. (1963). De quelques réformes des droits de la femme juive - a travers les âges. *Revue internationale de droit comparé, 15*(1), 55–61.

Guindon, A. (2014). *L'habillé et le nu : pour une éthique du vêtir et du denuder.* Ottawa: University of Ottawa Press [Les Presses de l'Université d'Ottawa].

Hamidi, 'A. (2008). *Maqāṣid al-qur'ān min tashrī' al-aḥkām* (Al-Tab'ah 1 ed.). Beirut: Dār Ibn Ḥazm lil-Ṭibā'ah wa-al-Nashr wa-al-Tawzī'.

Hasballah, 'A. (1987). *Usoul at-tashrī' al-islāmi.* Karachi: Idāara al-Qur'ān.

Herodote.net. (2016). *L'Antiquité à nos jours: L'esclavage, une realité qui dure.* Retrieved from https://www.herodote.net/De_l_Antiquite_a_nos_jours-synthese-16.php.

Ibn 'Abbās. (2008). *Great commentaries of the holy Qur'an (tafsīr ibn 'abbās).* London and Louisville, KY: Fons Vitae.

Ibn 'Ashūr, M. A. (2000). *Tafsīr ibn 'Ashūr, at-tahrīr wat-tanwir (verification and enlightenment), a 30 volume exegesis of the Qur'an.* Dar Ihya' Al-Turath.

Ibn Kathīr, Ismā'īl ibn 'Umar, ca. 1301–1373. (1960). *Tafsīr ibn kasīr.* Retrieved from http://catalog.hathitrust.org/Record/001926552.

Ibn Mājah, Muḥammad ibn Yazīd. (1998). *Sunan ibn mājah.* Lebanon: Retrieved from http://catalog.hathitrust.org/Record/003328127.

Ibn Rushd, Muhammad Ibn Ahmad. (1999). *Bidāyat al-mujtahid wa nihāyat al-muqtasid* [The distinguished jurist's primer] (I. K. Nyazee, Trans.). Garnet Publishing.

'Imara, M. (2002). *At-tahrīr al-islāmī lil-mar'a* [Islamic liberation of women] (aṭ-Ṭab'a 1 ed.). al-Qāhira (Cairo): Dār ash-Shurūq.

Izzat, H. R. (2009). *Lam yastawsū bin-nisā yā rasūlAllāh* [They did not take good care of the women, oh Prophet]. Retrieved from https://islamonline.net/.

Julien, M. (2010). *La mode hypersexualisée, une mode controversée * Sisphe.

Jumu'a (or Gomaa), Dr. Sheik 'Ali. (2008). *almar'a fī al-hadāra al-islāmiyya* [Women in Islamic civilization]. Dār as-Salām: Dār as-Salām.

Jumu'a, D. S. 'A.Taghyīr al-fatwā bi taghyīr az-zamān wa al-makān.

Lacroix, X. (1992). *Le corps de chair*. Paris: Ed. du Cerf.

Laham, H. (1989). *Min hady sūrat an-nisā'*. Ryad: Dār al-Hudā.

Laham, H. (2008). *Adhwā' hawla sūrat at-talāq* [Illuminations around the sūrah on divorce]. Damascus: Dār al-Hanān.

Lamrabet, A. (2004). *Aïsha, épouse du prophète ou l'islam au féminin*. France: Tawhid.

Lamrabet, A. (2007). *Le coran et les femmes: Une lecture de liberation*. France: Tawhid.

Laroui, A. (2008). *As-sunna wal-islāh*. Casablanca: Al-markaz ath-thaqāfī al-'arabī.

Lévi, I. (1904). *The hebrew text of the book of ecclesiasticus* [Sirach]. Leiden: Brill.

Mernissi, F. (2010). *Islam et démocratie*. Paris: Albin Michel, Espaces libres.

Müller, D. (2004). Bien commun, conflits d'intérêts et délibération éthique. *Éthique publique, 6*(1). https://doi.org/10.4000/ethiquepublique.2060.

Nasr, S. H., Dakake, M. M., Lumbard, J. E. B., Dagli, C. K., & Rustom, M. (2015). *The study Quran: A new translation and commentary*. New York: HarperOne.

Nisā'ī, Aḥmad ibn Shu'ayb. (1962). *Sunan-i nisā'i mutarjam*. Retrieved from http://catalog.hathitrust.org/Record/001404508.

Qurtubī, M. I. (1977). *Tafsīr al-qurṭubī*. Cairo: al-Hai'a al-Miṣrīya al-'Āmma li-l-Kitāb.

Qutb, S. (2015). *In the shade of the qur'ān: Surāh 4, al-nisā' (fī dhilāl al-qur'ān)* (A. Salahi, Trans.). The Islamic Foundation, 30 volumes.

Riḍā, M. R. (1947). *Tafsīr al-qur'ān al-ḥakīm al-mushtahar bi-ism tafsīr al-manār* [*wa-qad ishtamalat al-ajzā' al-khamsah al-ūlá minh 'alá jamī' māqarrarih al-shaykh muḥammad 'Abduh fimā alqāh min durūs at-tafsīr fī al-jāmi' al-azhar*]. Egypt. Retrieved from http://catalog.hathitrust.org/Record/001926732.

Sadruddin, Abū Tahar Alsalafi bin Mohammed. (2004). *Al-mashīkha al-baghdadiyya*, vol 23. Retrieved from http://shamela.ws/index.php/book/30093.

Salāh Ad-Dīn. (1999). *Mīrāth al-mar'a wa qadiyyat al-msāwāt* [Women's inheritance rights and the issue of equality]. Cairo: An-Nahda.

Saqr, N. A. (2001). *Manhaj al-imām al-ṭahir ibn 'Āshūr fī al-tafsīr, al-taḥrīr wa-al-tanwīr*. Alexandria, Egypt: al-Dār al-Miṣrīyah.

Shariati, A. (2009). *Fatima est fatima: L'idéal universel feminine*. Beirut: Albourag.

Stowasser, B. F. (1994). *Women in the Qur'an: Traditions, and interpretation* (Reissue ed.). Oxford, US: Oxford University Press.

Tantāwi, 'A. (1983). *Akhbār 'Umar wa akhbar 'Abdillah ibn 'Umar* (8th ed.). Beirut.

Tantāwi, M. S. (1992). *Al-tafsīr al-wasīt lil-qur'ān al-karīm*. Egypt. Retrieved from http://catalog.hathitrust.org/Record/002590648.

The Editors of the Encyclopedia Britannica. (2002). *Averroes*. Retrieved from http://www.britannica.com/Averroes.

INDEX

© The Editor(s) (if applicable) and The Author(s) 2018   193
A. Lamrabet, *Women and Men in the Qur'ān*,
https://doi.org/10.1007/978-3-319-78741-1

Druck:
Canon Deutschland Business Services GmbH
im Auftrag der KNV-Gruppe
Ferdinand-Jühlke-Str. 7
99095 Erfurt